BASELINE SELLING

How to Become a Sales Superstar by Using What You Already Know About the Game of Baseball

by
Dave Kurlan

authorHOUSE™

1663 LIBERTY DRIVE, SUITE 200
BLOOMINGTON, INDIANA 47403
(800) 839-8640
WWW.AUTHORHOUSE.COM

First published by AuthorHouse 11/22/05

ISBN: 1-4208-9568-0 (e)
ISBN: 1-4208-9567-2 (sc)
ISBN: 1-4208-9566-4 (dj)

Library of Congress Control Number: 2005909855

Printed in the United States of America
Bloomington, Indiana

This book is printed on acid-free paper.

DEDICATION

To my wife, Deborah, for her constant love, encouragement and support, and our son, Michael, for showing me that a (then) two-year old can do anything he is taught if the concept is simple enough. If it wasn't for Deborah's Tuesday night golf league, I may never have had the time to transport this book from my mind to my computer!

Acknowledgements

I would like to thank Deborah Penta, Chris Mott, Matt Hogan, Rick Cayer, Jim Sasena, Ed Kleinman, Steve Taback, Dan Caramanico, Terry Slattery, Tom Schaff, Chris Collias, Ken Leeser, Jim Lobaito, John Morrison Jr., Dr. Stephen Punzak, Fred Green, Rush Burkhardt, Marty Ferguson, Dan Lucas, Howard Bramson, and Rick Roberge for their feedback, suggestions, and time.

I would especially like to thank my two favorite authors: Dan Millman for his time, thoughts and ideas and Guy Kawasaki for hammering home the message that this book had better stand out from the glut of sales books on the market today.

This book would be a collection of rambling thoughts and ideas without structure and consistency if it wasn't for the work of my editors, Malcolm Campbell of Walkabout Press and David Weinbtraub. Their never-ending questions and suggestions really turned this into a readable book.

Despite the cliché that states the opposite, people will judge this book by its cover so I would like to thank the staff at PENTA Communications, Inc. for designing a thoughtful, eye-catching, yet appropriate cover that accurately depicts the theme of this book.

FOREWORD

Baseline Selling -- simple, readable, practical, actionable – a Grand Slam.

What more do you need to hear from the person writing the Foreword. In a way, to say more is just getting in the way of you reading the book and making more sales. After all, being a former sales and marketing manager and now owner of my own business (always selling!), the last thing I want to do is get in the way of a method to help you generate more sales!

As luck would have it, shortly after Dave asked me to write this Foreword I happened to have dinner with a good friend and colleague Tina Sung. In our conversation she brought up the word "minessence" – the ability to take complex ideas from different sources and convert them into a simplified, practical technology that improves society. "Technology" is used in its broadest sense to mean a usable practical system. Though you won't find the word in a dictionary, you will find a corresponding website.

Tina couldn't have found a better description for what Dave has created. Dave's highly usable and practical system for improving sales is drawn from the very best of different sales sources combined with his experience teaching and coaching sales. And he's framed his approach so it's both memorable and actionable – you can't use what you can't remember!

Having an edge in sales is always important and it's even more so now that the playing field has expanded globally. Most companies have optimized themselves about as much as they can. Now is the time to grab market share. At Gazelles we're pushing all our clients to get out there and sell, sell, sell.

And it's useful to remember that you sell to people, not companies. Selling is still a people to people process requiring a person to make a

ix

decision. As I read Dave's book I was reminded of many of the people fundamentals that tend to get lost in many formal sales methodologies.

If I say more I'll have to start quoting from the book. Turn the page and start improving your sales.

Verne Harnish, CEO
Gazelles Inc
Founder, Young Entrepreneurs' Organization

TABLE OF CONTENTS

Part Two: Getting to First Base

PREFACE

My love for the game of baseball began when I was a child growing up near Boston, where passion for the Red Sox bordered on religion. In 1964, when I was nine years old, my father took me to my first Boston Red Sox game at Fenway Park. I'd seen games on TV but the limited baseball broadcasts originated from a single black and white camera, far from the multi-camera, high-definition, full color images we enjoy today. Imagine the thrill I experienced sitting behind home plate, seeing the players up close and watching the pitches come racing over the plate.

The sights and sounds gave me a rush that I can recall even now. We ate hot dogs, ice cream sandwiches, and peanuts, dropping the shells at our feet. That year, the Red Sox were one of the worst teams in baseball, and they entered the ninth inning trailing the Los Angeles Angels 8–5. As the home team, they batted last and managed to load the bases with two outs. Tony Conigliaro—a local boy and the Red Sox young slugger—stepped to the plate.

He worked the count full. The game hung on the next pitch: a strike-out and the game would be over. Conigliaro swung at a pitch, fouling it into the stands. Twice more, he hit foul balls. The tension was thick. Those of us remaining in the stands were screaming for Tony to keep the rally going. We were slamming the empty seat bottoms along side of us to generate additional excitement.

The pitcher tried to blow a fastball right past Tony C, a nickname coined by the media. The fans, who called him Conig, were on their feet now, cheering him on. Unfazed, he took a mighty swing and connected. The ball soared deep into left field, high and majestic, until finally, it sailed directly over Fenway's famed 37-foot high "Green Monster" and landed softly in the net. The walk-off grand slam won the game by the score of 9–6. Dad and I, and every other person in the park that day, were screaming and clapping for what felt like hours.

Of course, a love affair with the Red Sox meant you learned to live with plenty of heartbreak—playoff-title and World Series losses—interrupted only by occasional euphoria when they won important or particularly close games. (As I write this—a full two months after the Red Sox broke an 86-year drought to sweep the St. Louis Cardinals in four games to win the 2004 World Series—I'm still excited.)

The same high and low emotions I experienced as a Red Sox fan have also marked my career in sales. It began in 1966 when, as an 11-year-old,

I sold greeting cards. Fortunately, during the past thirty-two years of professional selling, the joy of winning has far outpaced the agony of defeat. However, as with any endeavor, failure is a necessary component of success and I've learned a lot from losing.

In 1985, I added an exciting component to my career by becoming a professional sales trainer, and I've helped thousands of salespeople improve their skills and winning percentages during the past 20 years. However, I've never stopped trying to improve my training methods and this book is a testament to looking at your work in new ways. This brings me to my revelation:

Sales and baseball are very much alike.

At its heart, baseball is a simple game consisting of only forward motion. You advance through the bases in order—first, second, and third—before you score at home plate. Similarly, the sales process, when conducted properly, is also a forward progression of steps moving toward the close.

Of course, baseball and selling both have their challenges. In baseball, the opposing team tries to prevent you from scoring (as you try to prevent them from scoring); and in sales, you must not only identify prospects (that may try to prevent you from scoring), but also compete against other salespeople that may try to prevent you from scoring.

I have had tremendous success in sales and in training many salespeople to become outstanding performers, however, I've done this without making as complete a connection between baseball and sales as you'll find in this book.

I now see that my life-long fascination with the game was preparation for a career spent in sales and sales training. How so? Baseball has given me a new way to explain the all too easy to complicate sales process.

While I've used baseball as a metaphor for much of the sales process, it wasn't until 2004 that I realized the effectiveness of distilling the sales process down to a four-step process of running the bases—from home to first, first to second, second to third, and third to home.

Since my associates and I began teaching the four-step method described in **Baseline Selling**, our clients have been grasping the sales process much more quickly and, as a result, closing much more business.

If you're concerned that you won't "get it" because you don't understand—or even like—baseball, rest assured that this will not be a problem. This book provides everything you need to find more opportunities and convert them into sales because the concept is as simple as running the bases from home to first to second to third to home again.

So, warm up and prepare to play ball.

INTRODUCTION

My entire career—from age 11 when I sold greeting cards, to the present, has been in sales; I've never wanted to do anything else. I found the challenges and rewards of the sales profession so enjoyable that in 1985 I began professionally training salespeople. Training others has not only made me a better salesperson, but it's also been fulfilling to watch people become more effective at their profession.

Over the years, I've used and taught a variety of sales methodologies—feature-benefit selling, consultative selling, and relationship selling, among them—but I've always believed that there had to be an easier way to convey the steps necessary to make a sale, from prospecting to closing.

I decided to analyze all the great theories about sales, and reread many of the major books written about selling, motivation, and persuasion.

From such classics as Napoleon Hill's *Think and Grow Rich* (1937), Elmer Wheeler's *How to Sell Yourself to Others* (1946), Frank Bettger's *How I Raised Myself from Failure to Success in Selling* (1947), Dale Carnegie's *How to Win Friends and Influence People* (1936), and Dr. Norman Vincent Peale's *The Power of Positive Thinking* (1952) to more recent sales books, including *Spin Selling* by Neil Rackham (1988), *Solution Selling* (1994) by Michael Bosworth, Rob Jolles' *Customer Centered Selling* (1998), and Sharon Drew Morgen's *Selling with Integrity* (1999), I read these books and many more.

What did I learn?

All are excellent books and provide good information, but they added to my concern that most of the modern sales experts, authors, trainers, and consultants—and I include myself in all four groups—have unnecessarily complicated the sales process.

The systems, processes, and techniques taught today are complex and difficult to learn and apply. This is in contrast to the books written decades ago, which, while lacking sequential steps and such essential techniques as qualifying the buyer, had simple approaches that were easy to adopt and use.

The Numbers Tell the Story

You don't have to look far for proof that something's not working in the sales industry.

Objective Management Group, Inc., the industry-leading sales assessment firm, has tested more than a quarter-million salespeople in all ranges of experience and from every major industry. From 1990 to 2004, it compiled data and assessed sales capabilities with a predictive validity in the mid 90 percentile.

Figure 1 shows the percentage of salespeople, tested from 1990 to 2004, who fall into the various categories of performance.

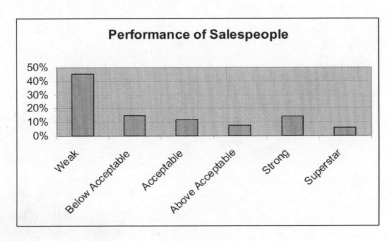

Figure 1

These findings are consistent with conventional wisdom regarding the existence of an elite group (6% in this instance) of sales performers. But the percentage of unacceptable performers far exceeds the 20 percent that traditional thinking placed in the bottom group of performers.

The bottom line?

Ineffective salespeople—weak and poor performers—make up a whopping 62 percent of the sales population.

Does experience matter? Surprisingly not. Of the 62 percent of salespeople falling into the *Weak* and *Below Acceptable* categories, 26 percent have been selling for at least 10 years; 44 percent have been selling for five years or more; 49 percent for at least four years; and 58 percent for at least three years.

What about training?

It is rare when a salesperson would be sent into the field without any preparation. The majority of salespeople in US Companies receive training from a number of sources, including in-house and third-party training; mentoring and coaching from their sales manager or another experienced individual in the company; and Internet-based and CD-ROM training. Sales professionals also tend to pursue self-improvement help. They read books by such experts as Tom Hopkins, Brian Tracy, and Zig Ziglar, and monitor trends and best practices from such industry magazines as *Selling Power.*

What Makes A Great Salesperson?

If experience and training—specifically, the sales training popular today—are not as influential as you'd expect, what predictors *do* impact a salesperson's success?

My research shows that the major differences between the top 26 percent—the successful sales professionals—and unsuccessful salespeople is limited primarily to hidden weaknesses, unconscious behaviors, and a lack of professional selling skills. As a result,

Good Salespeople Are Not Born. They're Trained.

Some salespeople are naturally gifted, especially when it comes to establishing rapport with prospects. However, don't mistake the gift for gab with the ability to develop a meaningful relationship. In fact, it's often more challenging to train an extrovert than an introvert to ask the right questions early in a relationship. Contrary to popular thinking, introverts make excellent salespeople, because they typically excel at listening, a great attribute in sales.

You can learn how to build rapport. How do I know? Because I did it. People skills did not come naturally to me, and I had to work hard developing relationships with prospects early on. (You'll learn ways to do this in chapter 6.) Even today, if I don't "turn on" my people skills, I will appear introverted, my natural state. However when I move into "relationship mode," people generally find me likeable, sincere, trustworthy and credible—important qualities to have early in and throughout the sales process.

most salespeople are unable to consistently and effectively execute their selling process.

Successful salespeople are confident in their abilities, understand the best ways to sell, and put those practices to work.

If you have the knowledge of how best to sell, but you fail to use your knowledge because you have too many hidden weaknesses—you will not be successful in sales.

Despite the fact that this makes plenty of sense, only 26 percent of us are "getting it." I wrote this book to help salespeople get it and get it quickly.

Meet AIDA: The Foundation for the Sales Process

In the 1950s, sales professionals began using the industry's first acronym to describe the components in the sales process: **AIDA**. To make a sale, you must first get the prospect's **Attention**. Next you must generate your prospect's **Interest** in your product or service; this builds the prospect's **Desire** to buy. The last component is getting the prospect to take **Action**, or making the sale.

AIDA's beauty is its simplicity. There are four stages, each of which is easy to remember. The problem is that AIDA is not a sales methodology. It lacks a process by which you move from attention through interest and desire to action. AIDA gives you the itinerary—the stops you'll make along the way—but not the road map, or directions for how to get from point A to point B.

It was with the popularization of AIDA that the modern history of professional sales began. From the itinerary, sales pioneers created various road maps, or different sales methodologies, to direct the salesperson through each stage of the selling process.

Where Training Left the Tracks: The Six Major Sales Methods

Today, there are six major sales methodologies, and AIDA forms the foundation for most of them. A complete analysis of the strengths and weaknesses of each system appears in Appendix B.

> This quick review demonstrates how the progression of methodologies from AIDA improved, yet at the same time, complicated the sales process.

The first methodology to develop, **Feature-Benefit Selling**, presents product or service features as benefits to the customer. The salesperson's objective is to close after the presentation. In a perfect world, it would be a two-step process—presentation and close. However, the product-centered nature of the presentation creates many opportunities for the prospect to raise objections, which can turn the sale into an endless cycle of presentation, handling objections, attempt to close, and back to handling objections again.

An advantage of feature-benefit selling is that the salesperson needs only a thorough understanding of the product and its benefits, plus bullet-proof skill at handling objections. Its shortcoming is the leeway it gives the prospect in raising objections.

Consultative Selling evolved next, with the addition of the qualifying process. Here, the salesperson acts as a consultant, by identifying the needs and problems of the prospect, and then presents his product or service as the solution to those needs. Made famous in 1965 by its sale to Xerox, the proprietary consultative selling system, Professional Selling Skills, or PSS, reigned supreme until the mid-1970s, when another consultative selling system, SPIN Selling, replaced PSS. Both systems utilize questions intended to cause discomfort, or create pain, as the motivation to buy. (See sidebar A Painful Moment in Sales History.)

Through questions, the salesperson demonstrates the costs of not using his product or service, and then uses a features-benefit presentation to close the sale. Because consultative selling focuses on the prospect's needs, tremendous urgency can be created while presenting the seller as an expert. The major draw-

A Painful Moment in Sales History

In 1946, sales pioneer Elmer Wheeler introduced the concept of pain as a buying motive in his book *How to Sell Yourself to Others*. Of course, he wasn't suggesting a forceful sales presentation; rather, if you can get your prospect to understand the impact of *not* solving a problem, you've created urgency for your product or service. Looks like your high-school gym teacher had it right all along: No Pain, No Gain.

back is the methodology's complexity. Depending upon which consultative-selling system you're using, the number of steps range from five to twelve, and the approach is very difficult to learn and execute.

In the 1970s, Miller-Heiman created and wrote the **Strategic Selling** methodology to provide a standard nomenclature for sales to major accounts. These sales cycles were typically quite long and involved numerous decision makers, or stakeholders. Strategic selling places significant emphasis on research as the sales process begins. The concept behind the methodology is that the more you know about all of the people within the prospective account—their roles and abilities to influence the decision—the more likely you are to make the sale.

It can be hard to get the various people in the decision making process to provide information about the company's needs. While it provides the strategies for success, it often lacks the tactics to make the strategy work.

Relationship Selling relies on the salesperson's ability to develop a genuine (versus superficial) relationship with the prospect through a series of "get-to-know-you-better" meetings. The concept is based on the belief that people prefer to do business with people they like, so the goal is to make friends first and sales later. As with strategic selling, the sales cycle tends to be long, so if you have time sensitivity, relationship selling will not work. It's hard to sell while building a relationship.

In the early 1980s, Michael Bosworth wrote **Solution Selling**, a methodology based on consultative selling. Like its counterpart consultative selling, Solution Selling starts with identifying pain and stressing solutions over products. It was intended to be used with hard-to-sell products and complex sales, as opposed to the transactional nature of other products and services. It differs from consultative methodologies when the focus is on proof and value justification as well as developing solution visions. It is difficult to learn because, taught in the context of complex sales, application tends to be foreign to those who don't have those challenges.

In the late 1990s, Michael Bosworth and other notable sales-trainers/authors moved toward the final methodology popular today, **Customer-Focused Selling**. (Books on this approach include Rob Jolles's *Customer Centered Selling*, and Sharon Drew Morgen's *Selling with Integrity*.)

Customer-focused selling emphasizes the salesperson placing all of her attention on the prospect's buying criteria and processes. It is a non-manipulative sales process, whereby the salesperson responds to the prospect's needs. Of course, the advantage of this process is that the prospect feels as if he is in control, but therein is also the disadvantage. If the salesperson is unable to regain control of the process at the appropriate time, she may lose the sale or be viewed by the prospect as merely a facilitator.

The evolution of the sales methods—from feature-benefit selling to the more complex systems that are popular today—has introduced good concepts and practices to move the process from attention through interest and desire to action. But that same evolution has unnecessarily complicated the process. The aforementioned systems require hundreds of hours of practice, dozens of unfamiliar techniques, the internalization of five to 12 steps, and memorization and understanding of countless terms.

That complexity is not a problem for the top 26 percent of sales performers, who will excel no matter what selling system they're using. However, what about the remaining 74 percent? For them, the six major sales methodologies are either too difficult to learn, take too long to implement, are ineffective and outdated, or are not used in the manner intended by their authors. The majority of salespeople will continue to struggle, as long as the approach is complex.

> **TIP:** Successful salespeople will be effective with any system or approach they use, and the remaining 74 percent will struggle, regardless of the method, if the method is complex.

Putting Sales Training Back on Track

What is needed is a new model for simplifying the sales process: one that's easy to learn, easy to remember, and easy to implement. Most importantly, the new model must be more effective than the current methods, or it will be of little use.

Introducing **Baseline Selling**, the easiest and most-effective sales methodology you'll ever use. The metaphor? Baseball. The terms? Baseball. The Process? The one you've known since your first kickball game at age five. Get to first. Get to second. Get to third. Score. In the upcoming chapters, I'll show you how to score early and often, raise your batting average, and have fun doing it.

Baseline Selling is easy because it distills selling down to a four-step process. It's easy to remember because each step is the equivalent of a base in baseball. It's easy to implement because I've provided simple techniques for running the bases that will work in every sales situation, every time. (Selling is selling, and anyone who tells you differently is trying to sell you on a more-complex system.)

But what about the effectiveness of Baseline Selling? Consider the results we've measured since introducing this method in our sales development business, David Kurlan & Associates, Inc.

Baseline Selling Gets Results

Two months after rolling out Baseline Selling to clients, we surveyed three random groups of 248 salespeople:

Group 1 = Salespeople exposed only to Baseline Selling

Group 2 = Salespeople exposed only to our previous methodology, a seven-step consultative selling program.

Group 3 = Salespeople that were exposed to both methodologies.

Baseline Selling proved 57 percent more effective than our previous consultative selling strategy in the participants' abilities to quickly recognize, remember, use, and get results.

The most dramatic difference was in salespeople's ability to remember and understand what the four steps represented. After only one day of training, 69 percent of trainees in Group 1 could recall and explain what each of the steps required, versus only 31 percent of the trainees in Group 2.

When salespeople are confident in their understanding of the system they're using, they will use it more consistently and they will sell more effectively. With only one day of exposure to Baseline Selling, 38 percent of respondents reported sales results directly attributable to the new method. One month after training, 76 percent of respondents said they could quantify sales results that came from the new process

Can you expect the same or even better results? Absolutely.

> **TIP:** When salespeople are confident in their understanding of the system they're using, they sell more effectively.

Who Should Read This Book

This book is for anyone in a sales or sales-management capacity. It's also for company owners, marketing managers, and client-service representatives. Such service professionals as accountants, attorneys, engineers, architects, and consultants will also benefit from it. Basically, Baseline Selling is for anyone who works with customers in any capacity, because the four-base process can be applied to any customer interaction.

Whether your company provides a service, manufactures a product, or re-sells another company's products or services, you'll learn the skills necessary to sell in a simple-to-understand, step-by-step manner that anyone can follow.

What if your company already adheres to a more complicated sales methodology? The Baseline Selling system can simplify any current methodology you're currently using. By overlaying the concepts and process I describe onto your current system, you'll gain a better understanding of what your current system is all about.

Knowledge is power. A better understanding of your sales process gives you confidence, lessens resistance from your prospects, and ultimately produces more revenue for you and your company.

Through, not To

Salespeople who will be most challenged applying this or any selling process to their businesses are those who sell through others. These are the salespeople who call on distributors, brokers, channels, and Value Added Resellers (VARs). As a rule, these salespeople do not sell directly to the people who will actually purchase their products or services. Some of these salespeople often have "manager" in their title. For the purpose of this discussion I will refer to them as channel managers, in an attempt to simplify the many nuances of these roles.

Channel managers often make a significant mistake when attempting to adopt a selling process for their businesses. They typically see the people they sell *through* as their customers, and start using the process on them. This is a mistake. In order to work effectively, any selling process needs to be used by the distributors, brokers, channels, or VARs on *their* prospects. This puts the channel manager in a training/coaching role rather than a selling role unless they are accompanying the reseller on a joint sales call. If you are a channel manager, what would happen if your resellers began using an effective process on their prospects? You would suddenly have more control over outcomes, something that may elude you today.

How the Book Works

In **Part One: Warming Up**, you'll learn the Four Bases of Selling, i.e., what each base is and what, in a nutshell, must happen to advance to the next base. In **Part Two: Getting to First Base**, you'll discover the simple, proven means of getting attention (**AIDA**) by prospecting and securing an appointment. As the most-challenging part of the sales process, I give considerable coverage to the obstacles you'll encounter in reaching first base and how to overcome them.

Part Three: Getting to Second Base presents the means by which you generate interest (**AIDA**) by determining your prospect's needs and problems, instilling desire (**AIDA**), and creating urgency. **Part Four: Getting to Third Base** covers thoroughly qualifying your prospect and your company to do business with one another. **Part Five: Running Home** drives the prospect to action (**AIDA**) with the easiest and most-effective close you'll ever use in sales.

For additional reference, you'll find a number of charts, definitions, and extra guidance located in the Appendices.

How best to begin improving your sales career? Turn the page and start reading.

PART ONE:
WARMING UP

CHAPTER 1: THE FOUR BASES

When Abner Doubleday invented baseball, he probably wasn't thinking about the sales process. But baseball sure makes a great metaphor for sales and selling.

First, it's the only major sport in which only forward progress is allowed: If you get a hit, you go from home plate to first base to second and third bases, before returning to home plate to score a run. All other major sports—football, basketball, hockey, and soccer—involve a pitched battle that moves back and forth on a field or rink. (OK, there's golf, another forward-only sport. However any sales system comprised of 18 sequential steps is probably doomed to failure from the outset.)

Second, look at the jargon of baseball and how much of it has found its way into the world of sales. Successful salespeople are "heavy hitters," and if you've failed to get an appointment with a prospect, you've "struck out." If you think about it, you're already using baseball as a metaphor for selling. (For more terms, see the sidebar Take Me Out to the Ballgame, and refer to Appendix C.)

Third, the baseball diamond is instantly recognizable, and the sales process can be likened to running the bases. The first time you hit a ball off of a batting tee and ran the wrong way, you were oriented to the concept of running the bases. Using the baseball diamond to illustrate the steps of sales and selling makes the sales process simple, understandable, executable, and powerful (see figure 2).

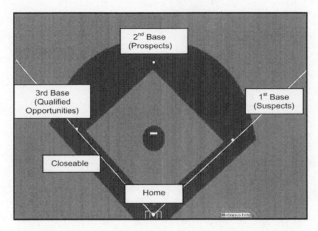

Figure 2

1ˢᵗ Base =   Have an appointment.

2ⁿᵈ Base =   They need what you have, there is urgency and you have shown speed on the bases (the S.O.B. Quality).

3ʳᵈ Base =   The prospect is completely qualified to do business with you and you are completely qualified to do business with the prospect.

Home =   You have presented a perfect solution, appropriate for their budget and they have made a decision to buy from you.

The Baseball Diamond and the Four Bases

What could be easier than describing the process of getting a first appointment—whether by cold calling, referral, or networking—with a new prospect as "getting to first base?" Reaching **first base** means you have a confirmed face-to-face or phone appointment for a specific time and place. But like a base runner, you've still got a long way to go.

You need to reach **second base**—that's when the prospect has a need and a compelling reason to buy the product or service you offer. To get to second base, you also have to earn the prospect's confidence by demonstrating what I call the Speed on the Bases (S.O.B. quality). I'll define that fully in chapter 6, but in a nutshell, it means you're likeable and have shown yourself to be capable and knowledgeable, and you stand-out from your competition.

From there it's on to **third base**, the result of having a prospect completely qualified. That means you know about their ability to buy, from whom they will buy, and why and when they will buy. Knowing this information plus the other factors I describe later will give you confidence that you'll get the business. Additionally to reach third base, your company must meet the prospect's criteria.

You only get to **home plate** when you present the prospect with the winning, cost-appropriate solution and close the deal. No matter what kind of sales you are in or what kind of sales methodology you are using, to close each sale and score, you must touch all four bases, in order, at some point in the sales process.

There are differences between baseball and sales, of course. In baseball, after you've reached base, you rely primarily on your teammates to move you around the bases; whereas in sales, the burden falls squarely on your shoulders. We won't be stealing any bases; we'll be awarded bases as we execute the sales process.

See Your Sales Pipeline on the Diamond

Another advantage of the baseball analogy is that you can use the

Take Me Out to the Ball Game

Here are a few baseball terms that have found their way into the language of sales and selling:

- "Bullpen," where pitchers warm up; describes the rows of tiny cubicles from which salespeople make cold calls.

- "Closer," a pitcher used in the final innings to (hopefully) win the game; describes a successful salesperson.

- "Hit a home run," knock the ball out of the park; used by salespeople to celebrate a successful sales call.

Some other baseball-oriented sales lingo: A salesperson asks a client "When would be a good time to touch base?" A prospect asks a new sales rep, "What's your pitch?" Salespeople are "in the field" whenever they are selling. After failing "to get to first base" with a new prospect, salespeople often say they "struck out." In sales, closing percentages are equated to batting averages, and top salespeople are referred to as "heavy hitters."

baseball diamond to represent where you are with any prospect at any given time. In this manner, you can see your entire pipeline—all of your opportunities in their various stages (shown visually, we can actually see the flow of the pipeline by observing where each opportunity is on their respective base paths) with the value, for the project/product/service/solution (see figure 3).

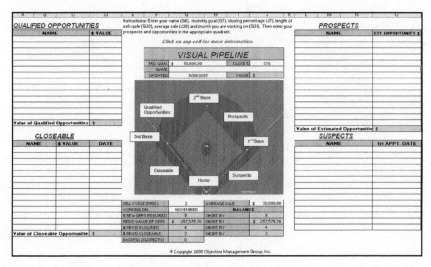

Figure 3

The pipeline must also be balanced; for instance, if you need 4 closeable opportunities at any given time, depending upon your conversion ratios, you may require 8 qualified opportunities, 12 prospects and 24 suspects in your pipeline. The pipeline also must show constant movement, with opportunities moving counter-clockwise around the diamond. And finally, your pipeline must meet a minimum financial value at all times, with enough new opportunities entering the pipeline to support your closing ratios.

Chapter Summary

Baseball is a natural metaphor for selling. The highs of closing big sales are like the highs you may have experienced as a kid when you won in baseball or any other sport. This book is about winning in sales by using the four bases on the baseball diamond to recognize, remember, use, and get results from a simple, four-step sales methodology.

If you're eager to advance to the next stage of your sales career, turn the page and let's hit some home runs!

CHAPTER 2: GOALS AND A GAME PLAN

When Babe Ruth would step to the plate and point to the outfield fence, he was defining his goal: to hit a home run. And he hit quite a few. Today, most major league ballplayers define game, season, and career goals. For example, a hitter might set his season goals as: to stay healthy, hit .300, hit 30 home runs, and drive in 100 runs. A pitcher might say he would like to stay healthy, win 20 games, pitch 200 innings, and finish with an ERA under 4.00.

Successful salespeople define goals as well, typically stated in sales volume, commissions earned or in more concrete terms like a new car or a family vacation. Setting goals is only half the work. Baseball players and salespeople alike also have to define *how* they're going to achieve their goals.

Think of goals as your destination and the sales plan as your itinerary to get there. When setting out on a driving trip, for example, you probably wouldn't leave home without a destination in mind and a road map. You use the road map to reach your destination in a timely manner without getting lost. Similarly, you'll use your sales plan to reach your goals within the time frame you set, and without getting sidetracked or winding up on a dead-end.

I can't overstate the importance of setting clearly defined, written goals and creating a written sales plan to achieve them. Here's a shocker: Despite the clear benefit, 83 percent of salespeople lack written goals and a sales plan!

What's the big deal? Selling takes vision and tenacity. Getting to first base is no easy task. If it were easy, everyone would be able to do it and few people would make much money, given all the successful competition. But the reality is that relatively few salespeople are consistently successful at reaching base. One reason is they lack the urgency to do the less glamorous part of selling—prospecting—every single day. This lack of urgency is the direct result of not having a plan derived from personal goals that dictates exactly what must be accomplished each day.

How I Learned the Importance of Goals and a Plan

I learned the importance of goals not from selling but from sports. I played baseball, but tennis was the sport at which I excelled. There was an annual Labor Day Tournament where, heading into the event, I was the second seed and my doubles partner—now a tennis pro and the former coach to Andre Agassi—was the top seed.

Before the tournament, I had it all figured out: I would dominate the rounds leading up to the finals and then my doubles partner would probably beat me in the finals.

However, when the tournament began, I played so poorly that I barely beat my first three opponents and ended up losing in the quarterfinals. That wasn't the outcome I'd imagined!

I was upset, humiliated, and felt like I'd let myself down. Sitting in the clubhouse and acting perfectly miserable, I caught the attention of John, the new club pro. "Is something wrong?" he asked. I whined my way through the day's events, and he sprang into action. I was about to get the lesson of my life!

John was a professional tennis player, recently off the pro tour after several knee surgeries. He said that I had great form, great talent, and great expectations but that I was mentally lazy. I protested, but he offered to prove it.

"You've seen me walk. I can't bend my right leg," he said, rolling up his pant leg to show scars like zipper marks that went in two different directions. "Here's what I'm going to do: I'll play against your two good legs with my one good leg and this racket," he said after reaching for a ridiculously warped wooden racket. (This was 1973 when wooden rackets were the preferred choice over clunky metal ones.) "How much are you willing to wager that you can beat me?"

Well, I thought this was free money. Here I was, a very good player and with a good racket. He was crippled and holding a racket with which you couldn't possibly hit a tennis ball. If I was mentally lazy, surely he was mentally crazy. I had $50 to play with, and he accepted my wager immediately.

He limped and I jogged onto the freshly groomed, green clay court on which I'd spent my youth playing. I served first, a hard serve inside the service court. Imagine my surprise when John set up like a human tripod, bracing himself with the warped wooden racket positioned so that the ball would just bounce back. He didn't even swing that ridiculous racket, instead allowing the ball to bounce back to me. I approached the net and pounded the ball to the other corner of the court, but John anticipated the move and was already there in tripod position, ready to let the ball bounce back to me.

So the play went. I would pound the ball, and he'd be there already set up, as if he had some Star Trek "Beam me up, Scotty" technology. Each time, the ball would bounce back to my side, until I'd get frustrated, make a mistake, and lose the point.

As the set progressed, about the only thing that changed was how long each point lasted. The volleys became fewer, my patience shorter, my frustration greater. By now, you can gather that this tour-hardened professional with one good leg and a warped racket beat me 6-0. I didn't even win a single point.

We returned to the clubhouse lounge, and after my embarrassment and anger subsided, he replayed the entire set—point for point and almost ball for ball—to explain everything I did mentally to get in my own way, raise my level of frustration, and eventually beat myself.

He went on to share the best lesson on goal setting that I would ever hear, and I've been teaching it ever since. "Your tournament goal was to get into the finals—nothing wrong with that," he said. "But you didn't have a more specific goal or a plan that you could execute. You have the skills, desire and good intentions; and you're a better player than the other players you met today. Without setting specific goals and making a plan to achieve them, you're being mentally lazy."

He said that before I could win a tournament, I had to win a match. Before I could win a match, I had to win a set. Before I could win a set, I had to win a game. Before I could win a game, I had to win a point. Before I could win a point, I had to return the ball one more time than my opponent did. And, most importantly, before I could return the ball one more time than my opponent could, I had to get to where the ball would be, set myself up, and be in a position to hit it before the ball arrived. He said, "And if you perfect that one thing—taking care of positioning, setting up, and executing—returning the ball where you want it to go—and do it consistently, you will beat everyone you ever play against!"

It was so simple—and it took time to get it right—but that lesson propelled my tennis game to the next level and formed the foundation of my future career in sales.

How does that lesson apply to you? Suppose your goal is to generate $1 million dollars a year in revenue. You can't generate $1 million dollars in revenue until you close a certain number of accounts. You can't close an account until you put yourself in a position to earn the account. You can't put yourself in a position to earn the account until you've been effective running the sales call. You can't effectively run the sales call until you've reached first base. You can't get to first base until you have a conversation with a decision maker, and you can't have a conversation with a decision maker until you pick up the phone and dial it.

> **TIP:** If you perfect that one thing—dialing the phone and having effective conversations with decision makers—and do it consistently, you will beat every competitor against whom you sell, no matter what industry you are in.

Setting Goals

You undoubtedly have things you'd like to achieve in your personal and professional life. For example, you might want to buy a home, send your children to college, save for retirement, go on vacation, or purchase a new car. You might also like to have more free time to pursue lifelong learning, hobbies, charity work, etc. All of these are examples of goals, which Webster's defines as "The end toward which effort is directed."

Whether consciously or not, setting goals is something everyone does, every day. Usually these are short-term goals that don't require a lot of thought: Finish the sales report, turn in receipts for expenses, and remember to pick up the laundry on the way home. At most, these "to do" items might require a sticky-note on your desk, or a reminder in your calendar or PDA. Major, long-term goals are like a glorified "to do" list, but with a lot more at stake. Consequently, they need to be treated more seriously than the average "to do" list.

Write it Down

Studies show that you are more likely to accomplish something if you write it down. Writing something down makes it "official," like a memo or a directive. You can refer to it later and see exactly what you meant. Written goals can be ordered and ranked, so you know which one to tackle first. And finally, if it is written down, you can mark it "done" when it's accomplished and move on to the next goal.

Make a Plan

A plan is a methodical series of steps that, if followed in sequence, produces a desired result. In the world of sales, this is called a sales plan: It defines what you do on a daily basis to achieve a goal or a series of goals. As with goals, a sales plan needs to be written down to be effective.

In addition to giving you essential direction, a written sales plan has several other important advantages. Like a road map, it prevents you from getting lost by ensuring that you'll follow the necessary steps—in sequence and in a timely fashion—to reach your goals.

Note that a sales plan is not the same as a sales methodology. The sales plan will help you reach your goals by putting you in a position to sell. The sales methodology is your plan *for* selling. Baseline Selling is a method that ensures you touch all the bases before you try to close. How? By giving you a step-by-step process to follow to get in "scoring position," or ready to close the deal. You can use the plan to check your progress.

The Plan Builds Momentum

In baseball, certain teams, batters, and/or pitchers often get into a groove and excel for short periods of time. Joe DiMaggio's 56-game hitting streak in 1941 and pitcher Orel Hershiser's streak of 59 consecutive scoreless in-

Daily Plan of Action

In baseball home plate is the site for the at bat and scoring a run -- it starts and finishes a successful plate appearance. In sales your plan of action for the day is the final step of the sales plan and the first step of the sales methodology – it too starts and finishes a successful plate appearance. The daily plan of action tells you how many prospects you must find, proposals you must make, conversations with decision makers you must have, and times you must dial the phone each day to succeed.

nings in 1988 are rare examples of long-lasting grooves that placed them in the record books. Of course, those streaks were built one performance at a time—each time DiMaggio swung the bat and each time Hershiser threw a pitch.

The most incredible streak, a record set quite recently, was Cal Ripken's 2,131 consecutive games played. Ripken's streak represents activity—the sales equivalent of making the calls. Momentum is an understatement in these cases.

Unlike most ballplayers, who are usually able to stay on a roll for only short periods of time, salespeople are often able to maintain that momentum for extended periods.

In sales, success generates momentum, and momentum keeps the success coming. Having a written sales plan helps you build and keep momentum by giving you a series of actions to take to keep your sales pipeline full. When you're committed to following your plan, the discipline of taking consistent action builds momentum for you.

Don't undervalue the importance of positive momentum in selling. I have witnessed many salespeople turn their careers around by developing behavioral momentum, i.e., consistently making the calls they have to make. When the wins finally come, their momentum is carrying them in two areas—finding *and* closing opportunities. If you fail to follow your plan you will find yourself without commission checks for several months while you regroup and literally begin rebuilding your pipeline from scratch.

> **TIP:** You build sales momentum by making phone calls, finding opportunities, and closing deals. These successes spur you on to make more calls, find more opportunities, and close more deals. Nothing generates momentum better than success, which as you guessed, comes from making those calls.

Here's a useful book on the topic: *Confidence: How Winning Streaks and Losing Streaks Begin and End,* by Harvard professor Rosabeth Moss Kanter. She says that from the simplest ball games to the most complicated business and political situations, the common element in winning is a basic truth about people: They rise to the occasion when leaders help them gain the confidence to do it.

Turn Around a Slump

Reverse momentum is even more powerful than positive momentum, as evidenced by the slumps that batters, pitchers, fielders, and teams all go through at one time or the other. It isn't uncommon for slumps to last several weeks. Salespeople are susceptible to both types of momentum, with one major difference: Salespeople who get on a roll seldom lose it overnight like ball players. A written plan, when followed, prevents slumps and, in case of a sales slump is the perfect medicine for slump-busting. It can be a reminder to get back to basics, keep it simple, do what has historically worked, use the law of averages, and refocus on the bigger goal.

In 1988 Al Williams wrote a book called *All You Can Do Is All You Can Do and All You Can Do is Enough.* The chapter entitled "You Can Do Anything for 30 Days" is a home run for any salesperson who is struggling. Williams discusses the things you can do for short periods of time, especially those you may not like or be comfortable with, knowing you don't have to do them forever. Then he identifies the little things that make a big difference in helping you pick up some quick wins, change your attitude, and feel better about yourself. Finally, he provides encouragement to salespeople who are failing, helping them to know that they aren't alone and that it doesn't have to be so painful.

How to Set a Goal and Write a Plan

So, how do you go about this magical step of pointing to the outfield fence and then stepping to the plate to knock the ball out of the park? The following five-step example builds on some powerful sales specific goal-setting principles taught by Paul J. Meyer. One of the first motivators to create a sales-specific goal-setting program, his 1960's recording, *The Power of Goal Setting,* is still available on CD. Follow these five steps and you will be well on your way.

#1. What would you like that you don't have now? Bigger house? Vacation home? Timeshare? Boat? Plane? Sports car? Country club membership? Home theater? New wardrobe? Special vacation? Private school for your children? Prestige? Career advancement? Promotion? The key is not to limit your thinking.

#2. Determine when you would like to achieve this goal and how much it will cost. Add this amount to your expenses to determine your required income.

#3. Figure out how much you must sell to earn your required income. Break this down into how many new accounts or sales are required each month.

#4. Determine, based on experience, what is required for you to close one new account or sale. How many proposals must you create in order to close one? How many new opportunities must you find in order to propose one? How many conversations must you have with decision makers in order to book one opportunity? How many times must you pick up the phone and dial it in order to have one conversation? Multiply these numbers by the number of new accounts or sales needed for the month.

#5. Figure out how many selling days you have available each month and divide the numbers in the previous section by the number of days available for selling. The results become your daily action plan.

Suppose you have 18 days per month available for selling. After doing the math, you might come up with the following daily action plan: dial the phone 47 times, speak with 13 decision makers and book two quality opportunities. You'll eventually propose to one of those opportunities and close one of every two proposals.

> **TIP:** Enlist the aid of your sales manager to hold you accountable to the daily action plan. If you don't have a sales manager, as in a professional services firm, or if your sales manager is too "hands-off" to hold you accountable, find another motivated professional and agree to hold each other accountable.

Distractions

Anyone and anything are capable of sidetracking someone who is vulnerable to being sidetracked. This is more about your personality, desire, and commitment than it is about the distractions themselves. (Sometimes, you may actually be relieved to be sidetracked, because this frees you, even if only temporarily, from a burdensome task.) You know what can get you off track. A certain phone call, a family problem, relationships, financial problems, rejection, the Internet, alcohol, drugs, food, gambling, laziness, a newspaper, sports, time off, friends, anger, fear, and paperwork are among the most common.

Make a list of all the distractions that could possibly sidetrack you. Now, write a prescription for preventing each one of them from causing you to abandon your sales plan and thereby deflecting you from your goals. It is about desire: How badly do you want to have greater success in sales? It is about commitment: Will you do whatever it takes to achieve greater sales success? It is about focus: Will you work the plan you created to reach your goals? It is about discipline: Can you consistently follow your plan without getting distracted? It is about momentum, getting on a roll, and maintaining a winning streak. It is about helping people solve their problems, making sales, and being paid handsomely for doing it. It is about having as much fun as a kid playing baseball.

It is about money, the ability to do the things you want in life, and the privilege of giving something back. Help others and show your appreciation for the success you have achieved. It is about leaving a legacy, being so successful that customers remember the impact you had on their businesses, and employers recalling the impact you had on their companies. It is about friends saying how much you enjoyed doing what you did, and family members saying that despite it all, you were there to enjoy every important moment and provide them with the best of everything.

When you can say that you've done all that, you can say you hit a home run in sales.

Reading Goals

Salespeople often ask me for additional reading suggestions for setting goals and making them happen. Several greats come to mind: Napoleon Hill's *Think and Grow Rich* covers goal-setting in great detail, and though his book is more than 70 years old, his thoughts and ideas are just as relevant today. Hill discusses the ways in which you must think, believe, and act in order for your goals and dreams to become a reality. Create your plan as I described and use his concepts to support the goals to which you aspire. Though Og Mandino's *The Greatest Salesman in the World* was the more popular book, his 1977 title, *The Greatest Miracle in the World,* includes extensive information about the power of goals, affirmations, and journaling. Chapter 19 in W. Clement Stone's 1962 book, *The Success System That Never Fails,* is based on the belief that the "most potent tool you can have in the steady pursuit of success is a written record of your daily habits." This allows you to "inspect what you expect." Read Norman Vincent Peale's *The Power of Positive Thinking,* a book he wrote in 1952. As a contrast to Napoleon Hill, Norman Vincent Peale provides insight to help overcome negative self-talk, the arch enemy of positive thinking. As you replace negative self-talk with positive thinking, you improve the odds of accomplishing your goals.

Two other audio titles worth a listen: Zig Ziglar's *Goals—How to Set Them, How to Reach Them* (Zig Ziglar is considered the modern day goal-setting guru) and Earl Nightingale's *The Strangest Secret,* both of which provide excellent suggestions on how to set and achieve goals.

Chapter Summary

Setting goals and creating a plan by itself guarantees nothing. However, if the goals motivate you to walk through walls and commit to your plan, follow it religiously, and build positive momentum, you will reach them. Want to better your chances even more? Tell everyone you know about your goals and your date for accomplishment, and the pressure will be on you to come through in the clutch. Remember that goals are simply motivating dreams with a date attached.

Now that you have an initial understanding of how I'll use the baseball analogy to introduce you to Baseline Selling, and you've had a primer on the importance of setting written goals and writing a sales plan to achieve them, let's turn our attention to where the sales process begins: getting to first base.

PART TWO:
GETTING TO FIRST BASE

Chapter 3: In the Zone— The Psychology of Sales

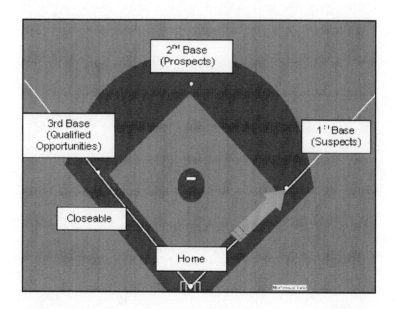

You know you've reached first base when you have a scheduled meeting (face to face or by phone) with your prospect.

When a major league baseball player steps to the plate, he's faced with a daunting task. Many pitchers can regularly throw the ball at speeds of more than ninety miles per hour. Not to mention the fact that major league pitchers can make the ball's flight as unpredictable as a tornado's path—both of which give the batter only a fraction of a second to decide whether to swing at a pitch or not. Batting in the big leagues is not the kind of situation you want to enter timidly or you're sure to strike out.

So it is with selling. When you step to the plate in sales, you want to have your game face on by being sure of yourself, confident in your product and presentation, and certain that your prospect needs the solution that you can provide. In short, you want to be "psyched to sell". This chapter will help you to prepare to step into the batter's box and be ready and excited to face the first pitch.

Salesmind

Selling, in its most basic form, involves one person talking to another: It's a form of communication. Your prospect has a problem, you have the solution. The sale takes place when you *communicate* your solution to your prospect, and the prospect *communicates* his or her willingness to accept your solution.

If only it was so easy.

In today's complex marketplace, sales and selling are fraught with the problems and pitfalls of interpersonal communication. Fears, misunderstandings, doubts, ego—all of these all come into play as the salesperson and the prospect try to reach a meeting of the minds.

> **TIP:** You cannot control your prospect's state of mind, but you can influence it by addressing and correcting your state of mind.

A salesperson who's mentally prepared for the rigors of the sales process has what I call a "salesmind." That is, she's overcome the common psychological challenges that prevent most salespeople from starting to sell. How do you develop a salesmind? By identifying, understanding, and overcoming the psychological obstacles that could prevent you from reaching first base.

Seven Challenges to Reaching First Base

Psychological challenges exist at every stage of the sales process; however, perhaps none more so than at the beginning, when you don't know what your prospect needs, let alone what her personality is like.

In my experience, most salespeople—no matter how confident—experience some form of fear at the beginning of the sales process. It may not be acknowledged; because experience has demonstrated that fear will not harm you. Or, it may be acknowledged and embraced as part of the process. Regardless, to be successful in sales, you must move past this fear and play the game.

There are seven primary psychological challenges to reaching first base: Need for Approval, Fear of Rejection, Call Anxiety, Negative Self-Talk, Perfectionism, Performance Anxiety, and Overbearing Ego. To some extent, everyone deals with these challenges both at work and in life. However, the degree to which they affect your happiness and impede your success is the measure of their severity.

If one or more of these psychological challenges (they often overlap) is preventing you from accomplishing critical tasks such as cold calling and follow through, then no new sales methodology can help you until you first address these fundamental barriers.

How do you determine if they're a problem for you, and if they are, what can you do about it?

The first step is to recognize the problem. Second, commit to overcoming these challenges. Nothing will change without your commitment. Finally, choose one challenge to work on at a time, and continue working on it until it's no longer an obstacle.

Challenge #1: Need for Approval

It's natural to want to be liked. However, if the need for prospects to like you prevents you from following or enacting your sales plan, you'll have a difficult time succeeding in sales.

The need for approval can have an impact throughout the sales process, but nowhere is it more debilitating than in the beginning, when you're trying to reach first base.

For example, what happens to the salesperson who, before calling a prospect, spends time worrying about how the prospect will not want to be interrupted by a cold call? She begins to believe that the prospect will not like her for this interruption, and as a result, decides not to call. When the need for approval prevents you from prospecting or from converting calls to appointments, you have a problem.

Solution

- Replace your need for approval with a need for respect. To gain the respect of others, it's imperative that you know why they will respect you: Expertise, integrity, authenticity, warmth, relevant curiosity, good listening skills and exceptional questioning skills. Seeking respect will cause you to perform quite differently than when you are seeking approval. Aretha Franklin said it best: "R-E-S-P-E-C-T. Find out what it means to me."

- Understand the consequences of your need for approval. For example, if you accept a high number of stalls and put-offs—prospects ask you to call back later, next week, or next month—you won't produce enough base hits (i.e., generate enough appointments) to score runs. Remember, second chances rarely materialize in sales. In my experience, salespeople accept stalls and put-offs because they don't want to appear "pushy"—they want to be liked. But by agreeing to call back at a later time, they fail to differentiate themselves from other salespeople calling on the prospect. That certainly won't get your prospect's approval.

    Remember, you're calling on the prospect because he might have a problem that you can solve. Ultimately, the only way to win his approval is to be persistent and polite, avoid stalls and put offs, and to get that appointment. If you fail to take some responsibility for solving his problem, the prospect's problem remains unsolved. (That won't get his approval.) By taking the stall, you don't have a prospect and you failed to get either of the things you were seeking: his approval and reaching first base. If you still think that seeking approval is helpful in selling, consider how this sounds: "I may not have reached first base, but at least the pitcher likes me." When you're looking for approval instead of business, everyone loses. We'll cover how to get on base in the next chapter. The important thing to remember is that an unhealthy need for approval will derail your sales success.

- Seek approval in your personal life, not at work. Have someone who loves you provide all the approval you need to get through the day, so you won't seek approval from your prospects. After all, what's a bad day at work when you return to a person who will affirm your worth, regardless of your daily toils? If you don't have someone in your life who can provide unlimited, unconditional love, get a golden retriever!

- Self-help authors can provide some insight on this problem too. I recommend reading *Your Erroneous Zones* by Dr. Wayne Dyer and *No Ordinary Moments: A Peaceful Warrior's Guide to Daily Life* by Dan Millman. Dyer has an uncanny ability to make self-help fun rather than threatening, and he does a great job on Need for Approval. Millman attacks Need for Approval from the spiritual side, helping to improve your life by removing Need for Approval.

- Use affirmations and self-hypnosis to overcome your need for approval. With the help of a hypnotherapist, Tisha Hallet, and her entrepreneurial husband, Norman, I provided the content for a wonderful CD called *Salesmind*. The CD/ROM, intended for computer use, uses self-hypnosis to overcome Need for Approval, Fear of Rejection, and eight other selling challenges. *Salesmind* is also available as an audio CD for use in the car where affirmations replace the self-hypnosis portion. (Not only is self-hypnosis a bad idea when driving, it probably won't stand up in court as an excuse for speeding: "Your Honor, this CD *told* me to speed.") See Appendix E for ordering information.

- Dan Millman shared a powerful exercise for eliminating need for approval. He suggests creating a shrine for the purpose of paying homage to a character he calls "Wuddle" as in "wuddle he think of me?" Each morning, before leaving for work, pay tribute to Wuddle by asking if you look good enough. Ask Wuddle if he likes you, if you please him, and if you are worthy of him. Later in the day, when you find yourself seeking a prospect's approval, you'll remember that you've already been through this today. Dan says you'll only have to perform this ritual for about a month or so before approval seeking ceases to be important.

Challenge #2: Fear of Rejection

The second biggest challenge is dealing with one of the certainties of the sales profession: rejection. If a prospect rejects you outright—by saying he's not interested, telling you not to call again, or hanging up on you—it's normal to feel bad. After all, you've been rejected.

But those feelings are only part of the problem. What's more important is how long it takes you to recover from feeling rejected. Salespeople who are back on the phone quickly and performing effectively have learned to deal with rejection. If, however, your recovery time takes several hours, or longer, before you're back working, your results will suffer.

The worst-case scenario occurs if this vicious cycle begins: The more rejection you receive, the longer you take to recover. The longer you take to recover, the less rejection you can handle and the more you begin to fear it. The more you fear rejection, the more you avoid situations where you may be rejected, like cold calling. As I've said again and again, if you stop cold calling, you will not succeed in sales until you have such a large and loyal customer base that you are receiving enough referrals and introductions to eliminate cold calling. What does it take to get there? Some more cold calling!

Solution

- Recognize the problem. How long does it take you to recover from rejection? If it's accounting for more than 15 minutes of your day, accept that your fear is preventing you from reaching your goals.

- Remind yourself that you're missing opportunities to realize your goals—that new car or Caribbean vacation—while you nurse your wounds.

- Recognize that rejection is not a rejection of you as a person. When a baseball player performs poorly, he may be booed by his hometown fans—not for who he is, but for his performance. When an opposing player comes to town, especially if his excellent play has beaten the home team before, he, too, will be booed. Similarly, you'll be booed in sales. What's important to remember is that the prospect is not rejecting you personally but rather any one of a number of things. Consider what she could be rejecting:

o The interruption

o The product or service

o The sales pitch – the fact that you are making a pitch at all

o Your script – the fact that you could be reading from an awful script

o The message – that if you buy the *XYZ* it will solve your *PDQ*

o Your claim – that you can do it better than *ABC* Company

o Your request for an appointment.

By accepting that the rejection is not directed at you, it's easier to move past fear and into action.

Challenge #3: Call Anxiety

A salesperson that avoids or procrastinates making prospecting calls suffers from Call Anxiety, a fear-driven state where he'll occupy himself with "warm calls," "busy work," and just about anything other than cold calling. Without dealing with his anxiety, this salesperson may push through and make some calls—he's got to keep his job, right?—but most prospects will sense his reluctance and inexperience, and in the best-case scenario, politely refuse to meet. (Worst-case scenarios—where the prospect doles out tremendous hostility—are, unfortunately, common.) Unless this salesperson gets a handle on his fear, or learns how to

The Value of Rejection

Bill Lee, a.k.a. the Spaceman, pitched in the major leagues from 1969 until 1978, and during one stretch, he racked up four straight 17-win seasons. He wrote three books of his own: His autobiography, *The Wrong Stuff, The Little Red (Sox) Book: A Revisionist History of the Boston Red Sox,* and *Have Glove Still Traveling: Stories of a Baseball Vagabond..* Speaking at an awards banquet I hosted, a salesperson asked Bill what he thought of rejection. Bill's response was perfect: "I think rejection is great. It's the most important element of the game. If you knew that every time you went out to play a game you were going to win, it wouldn't be any fun anymore. Who would want to play?"

present himself with confidence in spite of it, his case of Call Anxiety and inability to make cold calls could soon lead to a worse state: Job Interview Anxiety.

The best way for me to describe this malady is to explain Study Anxiety, the primary problem I experienced throughout my school years. I would read the chapter assigned to me and not remember a single fact from the pages just digested. Never having been taught a better way, I put the book down for the night, reasoning that I did the work but just couldn't remember anything. I would repeat this process, night after night, until coming to a powerful, time saving conclusion. I could get the same result in much less time if only I *didn't* read the assigned chapters. That mind-set gave way to a new nightly routine. I would bring the books home, look at them all stacked up and ask "why bother?" This powerful and rather successful (if you call avoiding homework successful) new twist on schoolwork gave way to my final accomplishment. Why bring the books home if I already know I won't be reading them? I had officially developed Study Anxiety. I know I wasn't the first and I surely wasn't the last but I sure did perfect it!

Solution

- The simplest, most direct way to overcome Call Anxiety is to partner with another salesperson who has the same discomfort. The plan is simple. Swap call lists and take turns dialing the phone. You dial the first number on his list and hand him the phone. Then he dials the first number on your list and hands you the phone. Usually, once you've each been forced to the phone a few times, the anxiety subsides and a friendly competition ensues instead.

- Call Anxiety comes from Need for Approval (Challenge #1), Fear of Rejection (Challenge #2) and Negative Self-Talk (challenge #4). By solving each of those problems individually you will eliminate your Call Anxiety.

Challenge #4: Negative Self-Talk

As its name suggests, Negative Self-Talk is making negative statements or thinking negative thoughts such as "I don't like making cold calls" and "I'm awful at prospecting." Whether these self-limiting beliefs stem from experience, the need for approval or fear of rejection, the end-result is the same: failure. Imagine a major league ball player stepping to the plate and telling himself, "I'm going to strike out!" What we say to ourselves has a lot to do with our success. As Richard Bach, author of *Jonathan Livingston Seagull*, said: "Argue for your limitations, and sure enough, they're yours."

Solution

- Recognition of your own negative self-talk can be difficult—until you start looking for it. Increase your awareness, identify your self-limiting beliefs, and rewrite them until they support your desired outcomes. For example, suppose you realize that you have been thinking, "He probably won't be interested, so I'll phone somebody else." Rephrase the statement to "I have the ability to interest him in what I am selling." After you have rewritten a number of these self-limiting beliefs, record them onto a cassette tape or CD, and play them continuously until the new beliefs have overtaken the old ones.

Challenge #5: Perfectionism

If you are one of the many perfectionists among us, you may have difficulty taking action until you're convinced you can do the job perfectly. Since cold calling has poor odds of success unless performed flawlessly, you can imagine how a perfectionist could have trouble ever getting this process started. But here's the irony: Perfectionists are often plagued by fear of failure, judging anything less than perfect to be a failure, yet even the best salespeople fail on a percentage of cold calls. So in a sense, success requires some degree of failure.

Solution

- Make a deal with yourself: Acknowledge that when it comes to selling and in this case, cold calling, you will be perfect at starting your calls at the scheduled time, dialing consistently and, most importantly, perfect at finishing the call. Since you cannot control the outcome, understand that the only way to fail is by not making the call.

- Dr. Kevin Leman, an entertaining author and expert on birth order, wrote the book *Growing Up First Born.* Because first-born children make up the greatest percentage of perfectionists, he devotes considerable coverage to perfectionism and provides great advice and suggestions for overcoming it. Get a copy of the book and you will thoroughly enjoy reading it.

Challenge #6: Performance Anxiety

Performance anxiety is a psychological challenge with physical symptoms. It usually precedes an important event—in this case, we're focusing on prospecting, but it also occurs before important meetings, presentations and closing, and it can cause the salesperson to botch his efforts.

Salespeople tend to follow their sales plans until they develop a physical feeling of discomfort. This feeling may be a pit in the stomach, a lump in the throat, the sweats, a rash, headache, twitching, or even a hot flash. A salesperson suffering performance anxiety allows these physical symptoms to provide an excuse to abandon his game plan or alter his strategy for a particular prospect or meeting.

I ask every salesperson I coach and train about the fun, exciting, invigorating activities in which they love to participate. Sports come up most often. So I ask them if, just before the start of the game or match, they ever get "butterflies." Every single person admits that they do and they come in the form of the very same symptoms I described in the last paragraph.

I always follow up with this question: "You get the same symptoms just before you start your game as you do just before you need to execute an important sales strategy. Why do you start the game but stop the sales strategy?"

Solution

- Recognize the symptoms for what they are—the sign that you're about to execute an exciting, important sales strategy with great opportunity for success. Recognizing them is the first step to turn fear and discomfort into action.

- Push through the discomfort. Remember: You could be just one question away from reaching first base or closing a sale. Imagine a cue card that says, "Okay here we go. This is what you practiced and prepared for. Now go for it!" Steve Farber, author of *Radical Leap*, calls these moments OS!M's or Oh Shit! Moments. He thinks they are wonderful, character-building events and a key to great leadership.

Challenge #7: Overbearing Ego

Everyone loves to be an expert, recognized for their ability to solve problems. In sales, pride and overbearing egos are prevalent, especially among salespeople involved in more complex sales. Such a salesperson shows his ego by his need to showcase his expertise.

Enter the prospect and the stage is set for a battle of egos, the loser of which will always be the salesperson. For example, when the salesperson-as-expert meets the prospect and immediately demonstrates his superior knowledge, the prospect can become intimidated, feel threatened, and may do something to prevent the salesperson from getting the business. If the salesperson attempts to correct a prospect who misstates the facts, the prospect may feel belittled. The salesperson wins the battle but loses the war.

Salespeople are notorious for their egos, but in my experience the most-successful sales professionals are those who recognize the power in humility.

Solution

- Develop a relationship. When a prospect is comfortable with you, he'll be more open to your ideas and suggestions. Don't rush to show him how much you know. Instead, choose to show you're interested in knowing him better.

- Practice restraint. You'll win your prospect's respect if you're able to share information with him in a way that empowers him in his own organization. Develop a partnership instead of a competition with your prospect.

- Ask Questions. The most effective way for harnessing your ego is to ask questions to demonstrate your expertise. The better your questions, the more respect a prospect will develop for you. For example, by asking "What would you be spending your time on if you didn't have this issue?" you're helping your prospect understand the consequences of a problem.

- Find gentle ways of correcting your prospects. In the 1936 book *The Psychology of Dealing with People,* author Wendell White suggested that, when correcting a prospect, the salesperson say, "I see that I did not make myself clear" or "I must have given you the wrong impression." Elmer Wheeler, who wrote the 1945 book *How to Sell Yourself to Others,* suggested that salespeople make an excuse for their prospects so they can save face. He suggested saying, "It's easy to make such a mistake." These suggestions are still appropriate today.

Chapter Summary

With a better understanding of the seven primary psychological challenges that can impede getting to first base and solutions to overcome them, it's now time to start the action. The next chapter explains how to actually reach base.

Chapter 4: The Sport of Prospecting

Can you remember in kickball or baseball, the first time you kicked or hit the ball but didn't know you were supposed to run to first base? Or maybe you can remember the first time you ran the bases the wrong way: What happened? You didn't reach first base.

One of the reasons so few salespeople are successful is that they know they're supposed to prospect, but they don't actually know how to do it effectively. They'll network and make cold calls but rarely reach base, because either they don't get the chance from the prospect or they don't recognize an opportunity when it arises.

In this chapter, you'll learn several ways to prospect—cold calling and making personal visits, networking, attending trade shows, and hosting promotional seminars—as well as the advantages and disadvantages of each. You'll also learn to recognize and overcome common prospecting obstacles. Finally, I'll share some simple approaches to help you realize the benefits from your increased prospecting efforts.

The Key to a Lucrative Sales Career

Closing is a game of percentages, and prospecting is a game of total numbers. The key to a lucrative sales career is creating a large number of qualified opportunities through prospecting.

You can't score in either sport—yes, selling is most certainly a sport!—unless you reach base. But getting on base—scheduling a meeting (face to face or by phone) with a prospect—is considered by many to be the most difficult part of selling. Why? Because of the seven psychological obstacles

Prospect Always

I am the CEO of my sales development company and the VP of the assessment company. I also take all of my phone calls—when I'm available. Some of the products and services the two companies buy include computers, office equipment and supplies, vehicles, accounting, banking, food, janitorial services, insurance, and legal services, to name a few. You'd think I'd be inundated with sales calls. Well, think again.

In the past 12 months I received a whopping total of six sales calls! One was from a salesperson (who received training from us) who tried to sell us new chairs for our training facility; one was from Minolta (I'm already a customer but the salesperson didn't know that) about replacing a high-speed color printer; one was from a commercial real-estate salesperson who wanted to know the expiration date of my lease (it was five years away); several calls were from MCI and AT&T; and one was from a guy who calls every year to get a donation for the local police charity.

Why so few calls? Several reasons: Some salespeople call too low in the company—they called on us but I never knew about it. (You should always call high up in the organization!) Some, who know I am a sales-development expert, are

covered in the previous chapter. Other issues like the lack of good prospecting skills, lack of urgency, discipline, and consistency also play an important role.

Just as a batter doesn't get a hit every time at bat, you won't score an appointment every time you prospect. Remember that in baseball, a great hitter bats around .300, or has success about 30 percent of the time. The same should hold true in selling. You might also want to remember that one of the greatest home-run hitters of all time, Babe Ruth, struck out more often than any other batter. You'll strike out plenty, too.

TIP: Closing a high percentage of a small number of opportunities is not, for most salespeople, the key to a lucrative career. Instead, the key is creating a large number of qualified opportunities and closing a good percentage of them. So, as you improve your prospecting skills, make sure you also intensify your prospecting efforts. See sidebar Prospect Always.

Four Prospecting Techniques

Many of the salespeople I've trained could already close a reasonable percentage of opportunities—once they had them. Their biggest problem was that most of them rarely did the work necessary to have enough opportunities to close! In training, I sharpened their closing skills, but more importantly, I helped them develop effective prospecting skills, providing them with more opportunities.

Selling begins when salespeople and prospects start talking, so let's turn to the various ways a dialogue can begin: promotional seminars, cold calls (phone calls and walk-ins), trade shows and networking. First, we'll cover networking, trade shows, and promotional seminars, and then devote the remainder of the chapter to successful cold-calling techniques.

Networking

Networking in sales is the baseball equivalent of the scouts that travel the countryside looking at high school and college players the team might consider drafting. Networking in the sales world means taking advantage of opportunities—professional gatherings, social events, and ties to friends and

afraid to call me. A few are targeting larger companies and justifiably *shouldn't* call on me. But most salespeople just fail to prospect on a regular basis!

family—to learn about potential prospects, and to have them learn about you.

When you have an effective "scouting" network of your own, you have a team in place looking for people who would be good prospects for you and your products or services.

The goal of a networking event is to receive more immediate introductions to people who could use your help.

It's important to note that personal prospecting, or cold calling, is the only activity *you* can control that leads directly to reaching base. As my great friend and colleague, Steve Taback, a noted sales development expert from Connecticut, says, "Networking equals Not Working." Of course, networking is important, but it is only a supplement to, not a replacement for, personal prospecting.

> **TIP:** The reality of networking is that you can't control any of the outcomes. Even with an enormous network of colleagues, partners, and acquaintances committed to funneling every sales opportunity your way, you can't plan for if, when, or how often that might happen.

> **TIP:** When you receive good referrals and introductions, you're in a good position to convert most into sales, providing you touch all the bases.

Trade Shows

Even good salespeople make mistakes at trade shows; here are some of them:

- Lack of goals. What are you hoping to accomplish at this show, other than to complain about the time spent out of the field and the lack of attendees? You should have goals for number of qualified leads, number of appointments booked, and new business generated.

- Lack of motivation. Don't wait for attendees to visit you! Work the crowd and entice attendees to stop by. It only takes a question or two to engage a passerby, and once engaged they should be very comfortable stopping to chat with you.

- Failure to qualify attendees. Once you have an attendee in the booth, ask questions to determine whether the attendee is a decision maker, a prospect, or a time-waster.

- Wasting time with the wrong people. The consequence of failing to qualify attendees? Every minute you spend with the wrong person is time unavailable for the right person.

- Wasting time with the right people. Even when you are aware that you have the right person at your booth, don't spend too much time with that person. The attendee has other booths to visit and you have other attendees to qualify. (Although trade shows are a great way to visit with current customers, you could miss many opportunities if you spend too much time with them.)

- Presenting. Salespeople just love to present, and shows are perfect venues for presenting—that's why the attendees come! Attendees learn what they need to learn from you, but you don't learn enough about them. As a result of the presenta-

How to Work a Room

Networking at an event can be an enjoyable way to socialize and sell at the same time. But how do you ensure you're not over-socializing and under-selling? Follow these suggestions:

- Always approach people rather than waiting for them to approach you. They will be relieved that they didn't have to go first.

- Instead of telling someone what you do, ask them what *they* do. They'll be pleased by the interest and excited to tell their story.

- If you meet a suitable prospect, ask them a question such as: "Do you ever have a problem with such and such?" If they say yes, ask for their business card, tell them you help people with exactly those sorts of problems, and ask if they would like you to call. If they are agreeable, ask when.

- If the person you are talking to isn't a suitable prospect, describe your typical customer or client. For example: "I work with the presidents of small to medium-sized, privately held growing companies." Then, explain the kinds of problems you solve and ask if they know anyone who fits your description. If the answer is yes, ask if they are willing to make an introduction on your behalf.

- If your product or service isn't appropriate for the person you're visiting with, don't overlook the value of offering a referral to help them. While it is usually more profitable to receive than to give, giving provides people with a reason to reciprocate.

tion, your follow-up call or visit is no longer needed.

- Failure to ask enough questions. All of that presenting prevents salespeople from asking the types of questions I recommend in the chapters on getting to first and second base (chapters 5, 6, and 7). How hard would it be to get an appointment with a prospect when you ask good, tough, timely questions?

- Trying to sell. Sell on a sales call. Attendees don't usually buy at shows—in most cases they learn what they wish to buy and then purchase at a later date. Your job is to make sure that you have an appointment to see or speak with interested prospects later.

- No plan for follow-up. Salespeople fail to book time in their calendars for the time-consuming job of performing follow-up calls after trade shows, a process that usually takes a few days of interruption-free calling.

- Failure to get permission. What good is a business card and phone number when you can't reach the decision maker? If you ask the right questions you can receive permission to follow up and assurances that you'll be able to get through.

Promotional Seminars

Promotional seminars, which include keynotes, workshops and executive briefings, can be quite powerful. Marketed and conducted effectively, these programs can place you in front of an audience of qualified decision makers who buy the products or services you sell. An effective promotional seminar is actually a carefully planned covert sales call disguised as an educational event.

Promotional seminars are perfect venues for salespeople offering enterprise solutions, professional services, and managed services. But don't rule promotional seminars out just because you sell commodities: Sponsoring this type of event will help differentiate your company from the competition (see sidebar Fascinating Fasteners).

Phone Calls and Walk-Ins

In this book, we'll treat cold calling by phone and by walking in equally. In most cases, the phone is a much better use of your time than unannounced walk-ins—you reach more prospects in less time—but there are exceptions. For example, if you're visiting a client, customer, or prospect, and have extra time before or after your scheduled meeting, it makes sense to walk to the next office, building, or home and make a prospecting call. That can be part of your reason for dropping in. The suggested dialogue that follows later in the chapter is suitable for both phone calls and for walking in.

How do you overcome the logistical barriers and get started?

Getting Ready, Getting Organized

Disorganization is often equated with a messy office, with piles of paper

Fascinating Fasteners

How can you create a promotional event around a commodity? Let's say you sell fasteners and most of the OEM's who purchase fasteners understand them completely. However, you want to develop relationships higher up in the company because you realize that selling fasteners to purchasing agents and buyers guarantees nothing except low margins.

Your ideal audience would be the engineers responsible for designing the products that *use* the fasteners. But how to attract them to a seminar? Connect your product to a concept that's important to the engineers. For example, I've never met an engineer who wasn't concerned with quality. Your challenge is to make the engineers aware of your commitment to quality, that anything less than a perfect fastener is unacceptable.

To create an event, you could hire a quality-control guru to deliver a presentation on the "Evolving Role Of Fasteners in the Quest For Quality." Hold the seminar at a first class hotel or an exclusive country club, include lunch, and voila: Your target audience will beat a path to your seminar. Tying your product to an educational event is something I call a Commodity Buster, or a means of differentiating yourself from the competition. (We'll discuss Commodity Busters in more detail in chapter 6).

and folders all over the place. But I'm often surprised how some sales professionals can work in a cluttered environment, fully aware of where everything is and able to locate what they need quickly. Conversely, I've seen plenty of salespeople who, despite immaculately kept offices and intricate filing systems, waste an inordinate amount of time looking for notes, files, and even office supplies.

Organization is measured less by appearance and more by how well you leverage your time. If you arrive in the office first thing in the morning ready to make prospecting calls but don't yet know who those prospects are, you're wasting valuable time. Or, if you're making follow-up calls to prospects but have failed to keep notes on previous conversations, you're wasting your time *and* the prospect's.

How can you organize your time most effectively for prospecting? Try these suggestions:

- Schedule time in your calendar each day for making phone calls. This time should not be interrupted. Treat the time as if it is an appointment with an important customer, do not accept incoming calls, respond to e-mails, or check your voice mail.

- Plan tomorrow's calls at the end of each day. There will be a number of prospects who must be called back from prior attempts or conversations; there are also new prospects you must call to meet tomorrow's goals. Make sure that you have a list of names and phone numbers ready to use the minute you walk into your office in the morning.

- Purchase contact-management software, such as **ACT!** (1-877-501-4496, *www.act.com*) or **Goldmine** (*www.frontrange.com/goldmine*) to help you track prospects and customers. Such programs allow you to record and take notes on every interaction as well as schedule follow-up actions.

- If you're chronically disorganized, you might consider taking a course from a company like **Franklin-Covey** (1-800-819-1812, *http://*

franklincovey.com) or **Priority Management Systems** (*www.priority-management.com*).

- Identify an extremely efficient, well-organized administrative assistant in the company and ask this individual to help you get organized.

- Hire your own assistant to help you get and remain organized.

> **TIP:** If you haven't developed a workable prospect list, rent or buy one. Numerous database companies, such as **Info USA** (1-800-321-0869, *www.infousa.com*) and **Zapdata** (1-800-590-0065, *http://zapdata.com*) rent and sell lists of prospects—including names, addresses, e-mails, and phone numbers—that meet your criteria, based on title, geographical area, and industry-specific information. Other companies, such as **Broadlook** (503-885-8063, *http://broadlook.com*), make it possible to import those lists into their software, so you can run live Internet lookups and get the most current intelligence needed to make an effective first call. The cost for these services is nominal compared to the dividends they'll pay in your prospecting efforts.

How to Be Effective on the Phone

The vast majority of salespeople are not prospecting for appointments on the phone *effectively*.

This wouldn't matter if you had an unlimited number of hours for cold-calling. But as important as prospecting is, your goal is to develop this discipline into a science, so it takes less of your time to convert cold calls into base hits.

When I first began making cold calls in 1973, I didn't have any of the required skills and I can honestly say I hated making the calls. I quickly realized that making cold calls to reach base took up a disproportionate percentage of my time. I would spend eight hours making cold calls just to spend three hours on appointments, something I found quite counter-productive. The more I cold called, the more I hated it. Finally it became apparent that I was spending all of this time because I was so awful at it.

If I became an expert, I figured that I could probably invert the percentages, get the cold calling completed in a relatively short amount of time and book more opportunities. I struck a deal with myself and agreed to work, tweak, and practice getting on base until I was great at it. Of course, by that time, I didn't mind doing it anymore because it was a productive use of my time.

The rest of this chapter explains various methods by which you can become a seasoned pro at prospecting. Using these suggestions, you'll be surprised at how quickly cold calling becomes an automatic, efficient part of your day.

> **TIP:** When you start reaching base regularly, you won't need to continue making as many cold calls. That's because more of your time will be spent running the bases, closing sales, developing a book of happy clients and customers, and reaping the benefits of all that effort in referrals, introductions, and repeat business.

How to Reach the Decision Makers

How often have you called a prospect only to be stonewalled by her executive assistant? These "gatekeepers" are especially adept when your prospect works in the executive offices. There are several schools of thought for getting past gatekeepers, none of which I've found to be particularly effective.

One is to become an ally, tell her the same things you would tell her boss, and get her to put you in her boss's calendar. The assumption is that the executive assistant knows the issues on which the boss is working and therefore can decide if it would be appropriate for the boss to meet with you. There are several problems with this approach.

The assistant probably doesn't entirely understand the underlying problems his boss faces, the consequences of those problems, and the urgency for solving those problems. If the gatekeeper places you on the decision maker's schedule, you probably have an "unqualified appointment," or a meeting that's likely to be a waste of time.

Another school of thought is that you should not tell the gatekeeper anything. Although this approach can work, most people can't pull it off because it requires them to be deceptive and withhold information, like the purpose of your call, in a way that doesn't get the gatekeeper upset.

Here's what I suggest: If you are calling high up in the organization and the boss is not available to take your call, ask for the boss' voice mail. Try, "Hi Mary, can you put me through to Bill's voice mail?"

Now you've nearly reached Bill, the executive with whom you'd like to speak. On his voice mail, leave a very simple message that he just must return: "Hi Bill, it's Dave Kurlan. As soon as you get a chance, please give me a call at 555-555-5555."

If you're calling lower in the organization, you shouldn't have any problem getting past the gatekeeper, if there is one, and a voice-mail message should sound very much the same as the one described above.

Why does this work? Because without the usual details, your prospect won't be able to ignore or discount the importance of your message. You could be a customer, prospect, vendor or potential partner. He has to return that call! The mistake that most salespeople make is leaving too much information.

TIP: The chances of getting a return call are inversely proportional to the number of details you leave in your message.

Phone Manners

Once you're on the phone with a prospect, nothing is more important to reaching base than how you sound. If a successful sales call were a formula, it would measure three parts phone manner, two parts mind-set and just one part phone script, or approach.

> **TIP:** How you sound on the phone is more important than what you say on the phone. (Although, of course you'll want to make sure your words work *for* you rather than against you.)

The most important aspect of phone manner is **tonality**, or how pleasing your voice sounds. (Most radio broadcasters have excellent tonality.) Tonality is a combination of many factors, including:

- **Warmth**. To convey warmth, speak with a reassuring, smooth, nurturing quality.

- **Sincerity**. Mean what you say, and sincerity comes though.

- **Pitch**. In general, lower pitch is better than higher.

- **Speed**. Depending upon where you are, you'll want to keep up with the region's pace. For example, in New York City and Boston, you'll be regarded as an outsider if you talk too slowly. If you're selling into rural New England, the South, or the Midwest, you'll be seen as in outsider if you talk too quickly. Generally speaking, slow it down.

- **Pace**. Break apart your thoughts by inserting pauses into your statements, separating the different thoughts for impact. This makes it easier to understand you and sounds less scripted. We will discuss pace in more detail in chapter 9, Ways to Reach Home.

- **Volume**. In general, the softer the better; however, pay attention to the geographic tendencies and adjust your volume accordingly.

When integrated, these components help your prospect to form an overall impression that encourages him to engage in conversation.

One of the biggest mistakes salespeople make when calling prospects is that they sound much too formal. I have strong feelings about this and always suggest that salespeople *not* use greetings such as "Good Morning", salutations like "Mr." and introductions such as "This is" during the call:

Such words create an instant sense that you don't know your prospect, must be making a cold call, and are therefore not important enough to speak with. The goal is to sound informal and conversational. Use the following words to start the conversation:

- *Hi or Hey (in the South)*

- *It's "your name"*

> **TIP:** Think of what you would say and how you would sound if you were calling your best friend to make after-work plans. This is the tone and style you should strive for.

Has this ever happened to you? Your prospect is giving you openings to which you can respond, but you are so busy trying to say what you planned to say that you miss them. Only after you failed to get a hit do you realize that you missed the opportunities. Not listening effectively is a common cause of failing to get an appointment.

Of all the challenges salespeople face, effective listening is perhaps the most difficult. Most people are "passive" listeners, meaning they "receive" when someone else is talking and "transmit" when their turn comes. But while they wait their turn, passive listeners are more occupied with what they're going to say and when they'll be able to say it, rather than what they are listening to. The result is they fail to engage in a true dialogue, thereby missing important aspects of what's said.

Tips for Active Listening

- Be prepared. You should be so familiar with what you need to say in your approach that you don't have to think about it at all. Be prepared to stop, jump, and go back and restart from anywhere in your approach. Master the thoughts, topics, suggestions, and questions you will use, so you can focus completely on how your prospect is responding to you.

Phone Tips

To improve your chances of getting on base, try the following:

- Act naturally; don't allow it to sound like you're reading from a script.

- Sound familiar, not formal.

- Ask permission to continue the conversation.

- Don't try to hit a home run, i.e., close the deal, on the phone.

- Be brief and to the point.

- Ask questions, especially those that can't be answered with a simple yes or no.

- Engage the prospect by asking about and listening to his needs and problems.

- Connect with the prospect, perhaps by finding a common interest.

- Understand your own business, i.e., how your products or services will solve your prospect's problem.

- Understand why prospects buy and what will motivate them to seek *your* solution to their problem.

- Know what you want to accomplish from every call; don't wing it!

- Clear your mind. Don't think ahead by worrying about what you'll say next, and don't think behind, worrying about what you or your prospect said a moment ago. Remain focused on how your prospect is responding to what you are saying right now. Your next response will be intuitive; you won't have to formulate it.

- Stay in the moment. Staying right here and right now is the single most important thing you can do to be effective in both baseball and selling. Don't think about the pitch you swung at and missed. Don't think about the pitch that you'll be thrown next. Pay attention to the pitch being thrown to you right here, right now, and how you must approach it. The more effectively you can perfect this art, the more consistently you will have success reaching base. Staying in the moment is the most effective way to clear your mind.

- Read Dan Millman's *Body, Mind Mastery—Creating Success in Sports and Life*. Substitute "salesperson" for his use of person, individual, or athlete. In this book, Millman shares exercises to help you master the art of clearing your mind, visualizing an outcome, and staying in the moment—or, as they say in sports, "in the zone."

I found that when I wasn't listening to a man attentively, I got my facts confused, lost track of the main issue and frequently came to wrong conclusions.—

Frank Bettger, *How I Raised Myself from Failure to Success in Selling*

Three Essentials Before You Pick Up the Phone

You now possess a better perspective of the required elements for effective prospecting. You've become better organized, set aside time for cold calling, identified obstacles that could set you back and learned how to be an effective, active listener. You've practiced your phone manners, so, you're ready to step to the plate and start, right?

Almost.

There are three essential elements you must grasp to become a heavy hitter in prospecting. You must understand your business, understand why people buy, and be determined not to give up. Let's examine these now.

#1. Understand Your Business

Salespeople usually understand the features and benefits of the products and services they sell. Most know what their companies do well and understand some of the added value they bring to the table. But what many salespeople fail to understand is how to translate what their company sells—the features and benefits that make their products and services outstanding—into words that will resonate with their intended prospects. Without understanding your company's products or services *through the prospect's eyes*, you lack a complete understanding of your business.

> **TIP:** Think of yourself not as a salesperson but as a problem solver. Your true business, whether you sell products or services, is to solve your prospect's problems.

In some sales scenarios, the prospect has an obvious problem and you know about it—for example, when water damages a property. In other cases, even the prospect doesn't yet know he has a problem. Whatever the case, in order to communicate your ability to provide a solution you must understand the prospect's problem from the prospect's point of view.

A great example of this comes from a company I'll call Quicker, Inc., which develops and sells advanced, high-tech software that helps patent attorneys search government databases to uncover both preexisting patents and potential violations of a company's existing patents.

The salesperson, George, knew the software, its features and benefits, and was adept at explaining to prospects what it could do. George also knew that his prospects already had software that did essentially the same thing, but that their current software had some serious limitations. Quicker, Inc.'s products did away with those limitations and did more comprehensive searches in far less time.

What did George do? He pointed out how much time his software saved by doing comprehensive searches—all true—without first helping his prospects understand the time they were wasting.

George learned that the patent attorneys had junior associates doing the research, so the decision makers weren't really in tune with how much time it took and how much labor was involved. George should have asked them about their process: What was involved, who was involved, how much time it took, the information this process revealed, and asked what everyone could be doing differently if they weren't spending all of this time identifying only a small percentage of the information they required.

George's problem, like that of so many salespeople, was his inability to see the prospect's problem *from the prospect's perspective*, and to communicate that to the prospect, without putting him on the defensive. (After all, the prospect presumably selected the current software after analyzing the available choices.)

Although George knew his prospect had a problem and his product could solve it, the prospect didn't know that (yet). Only *after* a comparison with George's superior software would the problem become evident to the prospect. Without the recognition of a problem, there is no compelling need to find a solution. In other words, if you aren't aware that your vision had become blurred, you wouldn't have any interest in new glasses.

> **TIP:** The key to understanding what business you are *really* in is your ability to understand your solutions from the prospect's point of view, rather than from your own. If you can't articulate the limitations of the prospect's current experience—with his current product or service—then you haven't yet discovered the best way to succeed in your business.

#2. Understand Why Prospects Buy

When you finally understand what business you are really in, you will have a much better chance of identifying why any particular prospect will buy. It will always be to solve their problem—one they may not know exists—when there is a compelling reason to do so.

If we take George's situation a step further, he failed to understand that his prospect didn't care about Quicker, Inc.'s newfangled software. They didn't care about the enhanced speed, expansive searching, enhanced features and superior user-interface. They were comfortable with the software they had. End of story?

No! George can close business by seeing the problem from the prospect's point of view and by learning why they will buy his software. He needs to analyze the prospect's experience and get the prospect to recognize the problems with the current software.

How might he do this? George and Quicker, Inc. have a solid record of helping other patent attorneys who were frustrated using the standard industry software. George can explain this to his prospects and then add specific details about how long searches take with the current software, how often the searches are incomplete and how they need to be manually refined. He can explain that his other clients were also frustrated over the number of times a search had to be rerun, since the standard software could not look for multiple variations of a search term. Finally, he could ask if his prospects have any of the same concerns. Having done this, he can make a connection with the prospect and get to first base.

> **TIP:** The method George learned to use, and you can use too, is a very non-threatening way to formulate likely user experiences into an approach that will be well received.

#3. Don't Give Up!

Before you start prospecting, you must resolve not to give up in your efforts, despite the certain rejection you'll encounter. In baseball, the batter doesn't give up when the count is 0 and 2, the pitcher doesn't give up when he's behind a couple of runs, and the team doesn't give up even when they're behind in the ninth inning. Yet, some salespeople find ingenious, time-consuming ways of essentially giving up before they even make it to first base.

Here are some of the ways salespeople inadvertently give up when trying to get on base:

- They send literature.
- They send letters of introduction.
- They take stalls and put-offs from prospects, such as "Call back later," "Send literature first," or "I'm not the right person for you to talk with."
- They go away when the prospect seems disinterested.
- They get screened out by allowing gatekeepers to do their jobs too effectively.

One problem shared by many salespeople is the inability to differentiate between a challenge and an obstacle. When prospects become difficult, most salespeople believe they have encountered an obstacle and fear they won't be able to overcome it. Successful salespeople, the top 26 percent, simply feel challenged when they encounter a difficult prospect. Rather than avoiding the obstacle, they back off a little, begin to ask non-threatening questions, and wait for the prospect to soften.

This is not significantly different from the battle that takes place between pitcher and batter. The pitcher attempts to throw a ball the batter can't hit, while the batter looks for a pitch he can clobber. If the batter sees the pitcher as an obstacle rather than as a challenge, he will undoubtedly fail.

Tips to Help You Avoid Giving Up

You may feel the urge to give up or take the path of least resistance, such as sending out letters of introduction rather than battling for the appointment. Use the following helpful tips to keep you on track and on your way to first base:

- Desire trumps all. When you're hell-bent on reaching first base, you won't bail out. Chris Mott, a talented sales development expert, colleague and friend, subscribes to the Babaji's Kriya Yoga website (*www.babaji.ca*) and shared this tip with me. It applies perfectly to prospecting. Weekly tip #118 says: *We should face life as warriors. It is not the nature of shakti (Sanskrit term meaning power) to be weak, timid or passive. When an obstacle appears, the nature of the shakti is to attack it aggressively. The shakti does not shrink back and cower. A person aligned with the shakti is courageous and is never on the defensive. Normally in life we retreat and we complain. We often complain about one thing or another. We have lost touch with our inner heroic nature.*

- Success breeds success. When you perfect your phoning skills and consistently reach first base, you won't feel the urge to give up and/or take the easy way out.

- Make it count. You only get one chance to reach base with each decision maker. You can either do what it takes to get on base or let the decision makers do what it takes to keep you off the bases. It is your choice as to whether or not you will get into scoring position.

- Read the signs. What happens if you've had a productive conversation and feel you should have reached base but are getting stalls and objections instead? Your prospects could be exhibiting their normal buying habits. Challenge your prospect by saying: "I understand that it's normal for you to try and get me to go away. However, I heard you say that you're actually frustrated with your situation and you'd like to fix it. So when would you like to invite me in to see if I can help you?"

Chapter Summary

You know the importance of regular prospecting and the various ways to prospect—cold calling, networking, attending trade shows, and hosting promotional seminars. You've learned more about each, with special attention paid to the most important prospecting method, cold calling. You've learned the importance of overcoming common obstacles including viewing those obstacles as challenges.

Equipped with this knowledge and these skills, it's time to step to the plate and start reaching base. In the next chapter, you'll learn how to turn your prospecting efforts into appointments.

Chapter 5: The Batter's Box—Reaching First Base

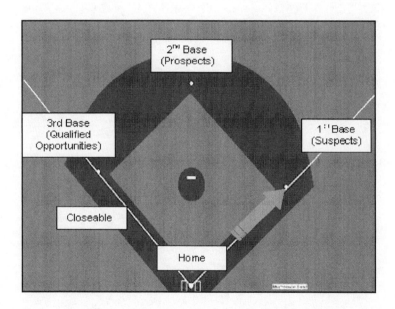

There are five ways to reach first base in baseball: You might hit a single. The pitcher might throw four balls, issuing you a walk. You might, if you are a feared hitter, draw an intentional walk. You could get lucky and reach on an error and, if you're hit by a pitch, you also reach first base.

It's time to move from the on-deck circle—where you've been warming up by identifying goals, writing a sales plan, understanding the psychology of sales, overcoming your challenges, and preparing your phone manner and approach—and step to the plate.

As you prepare to enter the batter's box, let's discuss the image you want to present as you step to the plate. This is called "plate demeanor." (Although I make the analogy between hitting against a pitcher and reaching first base with a prospect, I am not proposing that your prospect is actually an opponent, although early in the first conversation it may sometimes appear that way.)

Plate Demeanor

When a batter steps to the plate, his plate appearance, or the character he projects, will be an important part of his success at bat. Successful salespeople must begin the sales process with an equally strong plate appearance. Salespeople and good batters share the following attributes when they step to the plate:

- Presence. Both batter and salesperson carry themselves with a certain presence. They look, act, sound, and feel successful. Successful salespeople have a quiet confidence about them, a warm, reassuring smile, a calming manner and a professional appearance.

- Patience. Ted Williams, perhaps baseball's greatest hitter of all time, said the key to hitting is having the patience to wait for a pitch you can handle, rather than swinging at a pitcher's pitch. The same holds true in selling, where you must have the patience to wait for the prospect to give you an opening—an opportunity for you to say or ask something that will help you reach base. In baseball, the first pitch might not be the one you swing at, and in selling it may take several exchanges between you and your prospect before you have the appropriate opportunity to make your move. Don't get too anxious, don't swing for the sake of swinging, and remember: On every call, there will usually be at least one opportunity to reach base.

- Confidence. You must be eternally optimistic about your outcome. That is confidence. But you must be realistic about what you are likely to encounter along the way. If you are *certain* you will meet resistance, but *confident* about your ability to handle that resistance and achieve your outcome, you can proceed with all the internal optimism you can muster.

- Discernment. A batter's creed is not to do more with the pitch than is possible. In sales, the philosophy is the same: Don't try to do more with the call than you have the opportunity to do. If the prospect has only a single issue on which you can help, now is not the time to introduce other areas for which he does not immediately have a need.

Five Ways to Reach First Base

Remember, reaching first base was defined in chapter 1 as the process of getting a first appointment with a prospect. Let's look at the five ways you can reach first base.

#1. Hit a single

In sales, you must not try to hit a home run over the phone, when all you have to do is reach base. If you attempt to do too much in a short phone conversation, you will likely complicate matters enough so that you don't reach base at all. A knock on home-run hitters is that they too often *try* to hit home runs, and end up striking out. So don't try to hit it out of the park, just get on base.

#2. Walk

When you receive an introduction or a strong referral from one of your customers, clients, or centers of influence it will usually get you invited in to see your prospect. We'll call that the sales equivalent of a walk—something at which you should strive to become a specialist. A walk is considered as good as a hit in baseball, and you should come to treasure walks in selling as well. The most feared batters in baseball walk more than anyone else in the game. A salesperson who effectively services his customers and clients, and consistently stays in touch with his networks, resources, and friends, will draw a great number of walks.

#3. Intentional walk

In baseball, when the hitting team has runners in scoring position and first base is open, the opposing team may intentionally walk the next batter if they respect his ability to hit in the clutch. This prevents the batter from driving in a run; allows the pitcher to face a batter he may be able to handle more easily; and sets up a force play at second base. If your prospect is in a jam, you may receive an intentional walk when he invites you in because he respects your ability to solve problems. When he asks if you can help, you have not only reached base via an intentional walk, you have a huge advantage over your competitors.

#4 Hit by the pitch

When the prospect phones you before you get around to calling her, that's the sales equivalent of getting hit by the pitch—you get a free pass to first base. But just like in baseball, you could be bruised up a bit, i.e., you'll probably have competition. That's because although this prospect did call you, she probably called many of your competitors as well. (This calls for special base-running skills, something we'll cover in the next chapter.)

#5 Reached on an error

In baseball, the batter could reach base when his opponent makes a mistake. In sales, you may reach base when you get a Request for a Proposal (RFP) or Request for a Quote (RFQ). Just like in baseball, you'll need to take advantage of these opportunities when they come your way. We will discuss this further in chapter 9, Ways to Reach Home.

> **TIP:** On Base Percentage (OBP) is becoming a more important part of baseball than batting average (although the batters with the higher batting averages are still compensated with higher salaries). In sales we are also more interested in getting on base than we are with whether you do so by a hit, a walk, being hit by a pitch or reaching on an error. Remember, you can't score, or win, unless you get on base.

Hitting a Single

In baseball, when you connect with the ball and "hit it where they ain't," you are assured of at least a single. When you make a connection on the phone, ask the right questions, and get an appointment, you've hit a single in sales. The key to reaching first base via a single is your ability to ask two questions at some point during the short initial phone conversation: 1) "Is it a problem?" and 2) "Would you like to fix it?"

A "yes" answer to those two questions allows you to book an appointment that will be scored a single and you'll be standing proudly on first base. So what must you say and ask during this phone conversation in order to get to those two questions?

First, think about your business, your products, and your services. Second, think about your prospect's business, and the possible issues your prospect might have that would qualify as problems you could solve. Third, think about the way your solutions solve your prospect's problems. As we discussed in chapter 4, when you think about your business and your prospect's experiences in this way, you'll find it easier to reach base.

In sales, the key to reaching first base is to know your prospects. When you have information about their challenges, problems, likes, and dislikes, your opening statement and initial questions will have more impact.

In baseball, each team has a staff of advance scouts who spend the entire season traveling and watching the teams that will be upcoming opponents. Scouting reports help the fielders to be better positioned on defense when they take the field. They help pitchers to be more aware of opposing batters' weaknesses and they help batters have a better sense of what to expect at the plate in terms of type, location, and speed of pitches. Based on the scouting reports, the team can develop a plan to win by getting runners on base and preventing opponents from scoring.

There are four types of messages a salesperson may hear *from* a prospect while trying to get to first base: Symptoms, Problems, Reactions, and Consequences. Hearing any one (or more) of these messages during the phone call should enable the salesperson to reach first base. Why? Because it allows the salesperson to ask those two key questions: 1) "Is it a problem?" and 2) "Would you like to fix it?" The key to recognizing these four types of messages will be your ability to listen effectively. The following examples place the four messages in context.

#1. Symptoms. Your prospect may begin the call by sharing a symptom that might be indicative of a problem, but not the actual problem. For instance, he might tell a contractor that his basement is flooded. Although that might be the problem from the prospect's perspective, it is not the *real* problem. The contractor might say that the foundation has a crack, the yard is not properly graded, the water from the storm drain is not being adequately diverted from the house, the bath upstairs is leaking, there is a broken water main, etc. One of those issues will be the real problem.

#2. Problems. When the contractor tells the prospect that the water main has burst and the entire yard, foundation, and basement floor must be dug up, the prospect learns about the real problem for the first time.

#3. Reactions. The prospect's reaction to the problem will likely take the form of frustration, horror, anger, fear, or anxiety, guilt, greed, jealousy, and envy.

#4. Consequences. The consequences are what will happen if the prospect doesn't fix the problem. His entire basement will fill up with water, the yard will become the neighborhood pond, everything in the basement will be ruined, the family won't be able to cook with water or take showers or baths, and the value of their home will drop like a rock.

Now that you have a sense for what the four messages might sound like, let's discuss what it will take for you to reach first base consistently.

Six Exercises to Help You Reach Base

#1. Create a list of problems that you, your products, or services address. Rather than a list of services you provide, list the problems those services solve.

#2. List all of the problems you've ever heard about from your prospects.

#3. Indicate whether each problem is really the problem itself, the symptom of the problem, or your prospect's reaction to the problem.

#4. Create a list of symptoms that would lead you to identify a real problem.

#5. Create a list of reactions that someone experiencing these problems would likely have.

#6. If there are consequences, i.e., a price to be paid, for *not* solving these problems, add the consequences to your list.

To make the results of this exercise easier to use, and to improve your odds of getting on base more frequently, create a table similar to the one in figure 4. The table has four columns: Symptom, Problem, Reaction, Consequences. This table simply takes symptoms that you hear on a regular basis and asks you to determine three things: the real problem behind the symptom, the reaction you would expect from a prospect with such a problem, and the consequences if the problem remains unsolved.

Table of Symptoms, Problems, Reactions, and Consequences

Symptom	Problem	Reaction	Consequences

Figure 4

Three Approaches to Help You Get on Base

The previous six exercises help you develop the information you will need as you're stepping up to the plate, and the table in figure 4 provides a way to organize the information effectively. Next we'll look at three approaches to help you reach base: the positioning statement, self-referral, and interview.

The Positioning Statement

With this approach, you use a positioning statement—a short, declarative sentence that describes your business—to tell a prospect about the problems you solve. Then, you ask your prospect if he has any problems of that kind. A positioning statement must accomplish three things *in as few words as possible*. First, it must tell your prospect what you do. Second, it must connect what you do with the prospect's likely experiences and needs. Third, there must be a very good chance your prospect will respond by thinking, "That's me" or "That's us." Remember, the goal is to direct the conversation to the point where you can ask the two key questions: "Is that a problem?" and "Do you want to fix it?"

To put all this in perspective, let me relate an exercise I conducted for American Electrical Testing for the purpose of helping them create its positioning statements.

We started by identifying the company's various markets and narrowing the company's sales focus so that only desirable, profitable markets were being targeted. Salespeople have a tendency to call where they are comfortable, rather than where the company is best positioned for success.

Next, we created a table like the one in figure 5. The table has one column for each target market, a column for the issues we could discuss to connect with decision makers, and a column to describe their reaction to the problem. Finally, we reviewed each issue and the impact on the decision makers in each market. This allowed us to identify the statements that were both powerful and likely to evoke agreement. (I've added a seventh column to show you which statements were ultimately chosen.)

Table for American Electrical Testing

Legend
MCEU = Mission Critical End User
T & D Prov. = Transmission and Distribution Provider
T & D Contr. = Transmission and Distribution Contractor
Util. Gen = Utility that Generates Electricity

MCEU	T & D Provider	T & D Contractor	Utility Generator	Issue	Reaction	Utilized
X	X	X	X	Unexpected Failure	Fear	No
X			X	Inability to resolve chronic problems	Frustration	No
	X	X	X	Penalties	Hurt	No
X	X		X	Inevitable catastrophic failure	Fear	No
X	X	X	X	Inability to meet maintenance and testing requirements	Pressure	Yes
	X			Inability to earn rate increases	Frustration	No
X			X	Lack of qualified emergency staff	Oh Shit Moments	Yes
		X	X	Poor choice of high voltage subs	Burned	Yes
X			X	Lack of high voltage experience among electricians	Frustrated	No
X	X	X	X	Economic loss	Suffered	No
X	X	X	x	Inability to meet deadlines	Stressed	No

Figure 5

Let's use one of the issues we chose and translate it into a positioning statement. The chosen issue is "Lack of qualified emergency staff." The target industry is utility generators. They'll be calling on plant managers, because they are the decision makers for staffing issues. Here's the positioning statement we developed: I help Plant Managers who have had one too many "Oh shit!" moments when they needed, but didn't have, qualified emergency staff." (The salty language is appropriate for a plant manager but I would advise against using similar language when calling on a white collar executive.)

Now let's use the positioning statement in a cold sales call:

You:	Hi John, it's Dave Kurlan. (Stop and wait for response.)
Prospect:	Yes Dave?
You:	It doesn't sound like you know who I am. Can I tell you why I called?
Prospect:	Sure.
You:	I help plant managers who have had one too many "Oh shit!" moments when they needed, but didn't have, qualified emergency staff. Can I ask you a question?
Prospect:	Sure.
You:	How often does that happen in your company?
Prospect:	A couple of times a year.
You:	Is that a lot?
Prospect:	A couple of times more than we would like.
You:	Is that a problem?
Prospect:	Yes.
You:	Would you like to fix it?
Prospect:	Yes
You:	When would you like to invite me in to see if I can help?

Self-Referral

This approach allows you to short-cut the referral process. Instead of waiting for a satisfied customer to refer you to a prospect, you approach qualified prospects and tell them how you have created satisfied customers by solving problems similar to theirs. Using this approach allows you to tell a prospect about the problems you have been solving for others, and to ask if he would like to invite you in to hear about how you have helped them and how you might help him.

Here's how a self-referral call might sound:

You:	Hi John, it's Dave Kurlan. (Stop and wait for response.)
Prospect:	Yes Dave?
You:	It doesn't sound like you know who I am. Can I tell you why I called?
Prospect:	Sure.
You:	I've been very successful helping plant managers who have had one too many "Oh shit!" moments when they needed, but didn't have, qualified emergency staff. I thought you might want to invite me in to learn more about how I have helped other plant managers and how I might be able to help you with issues like those.
Prospect:	OK.

Interview

This approach gets you an appointment with a prospect, not to make a sales call, but to conduct an interview. Most people feel flattered when asked if they would agree to be interviewed, whether for a book, a magazine, a newsletter or a newspaper. The caveat here is that you must actually be writing something for which a prospect would have an opinion or a potential contribution. This is not as far-fetched as it sounds. There are many publications that deal with business, including business magazines, trade publications, business sections of daily newspapers, chambers of commerce newsletters, etc. You can even publish your own newsletter. What makes this approach so potentially rewarding is that your customers and prospects probably read these publications. So, not only do you get in to see your immediate prospect, you increase both his and your visibility and prestige in the business community at large.

Here's an example of a phone call to set up an interview:

You: Hi John, it's Dave Kurlan.
             (Stop and wait for response.)

Prospect: Hi, Dave.

You: Oh, good. It sounds like you know who I am. Can I tell you why I called?

Prospect: Sure.

You: I'm writing an article for *Quality Control Journal* on plant managers who have had one too many "Oh shit!" moments when they needed, but didn't have, qualified emergency staff. I was hoping that as a local plant manager, you would agree to be interviewed for my article.

Prospect: OK.

Make sure that your interview questions deal with the prospect's likely problems and then, at the end of the interview, simply ask your prospect if he would like some help solving the problems he shared with you.

Slow Motion Replay

Let's analyze the shared elements of the three previous phone approaches—the greeting, stop sign, and request to continue—to make sure that this call works as well for you as it does for others who use it successfully.

You can listen to a sample phone call at

http://www.baselineselling.com

where you can have positioning statements professionally created for you.

- The Greeting. When you say, "Hi John (or Sue, or Mike), it's Dave Kurlan" it is imperative that you sound like the prospect's best friend. You should imitate the way you sound when you phone your best friend to invite him or her to a special event. When you sound that familiar and uplifting, your prospect will want to speak with you. You can influence this by using your tonality effectively, making sure that you sound friendly, warm, and outgoing. This greeting is the single most important thing you will say in your attempt to reach first base, so practice your opening line again and again until it sounds the same as when you call your best friend.

- The stop sign. Next, make sure you obey the stop sign. In baseball a first base coach tells you whether to run or stop at first base. After you've stated your name, you must refrain from saying anything else until your prospect has responded. The purpose of this is to take his attention away from the work he was doing and get him to focus on you for just a moment.

- Ask permission. Finally, before you can continue with your dialogue, you must get permission to continue. Permission is necessary so that the prospect understands that you respect his time and so you know that he has agreed to speak with you. You will be asking permission throughout the sales process. Sometimes, you'll simply ask, "Can we talk some more about that?" Other times you might ask, "Is it OK if we talk about how that's working?" It is very subtle but very important to ask permission in this manner. Each time your prospect grants permission they are saying "yes" to you so it's also very good practice for them.

A Good At Bat

Some of your calls will result in easily reaching base while others will clearly be strikeouts. It is important to remember that in baseball, a great hitter bats around .300 or has success about 30 percent of the time. The same should hold true in selling. You should also remember that one of the greatest home-run hitters of all time, Babe Ruth, struck out more often than any other hitter. You will strikeout too.

In baseball, a batter who forces the pitcher to throw a lot of pitches, fouls a number of balls off, and finally reaches base is considered to have had a good at bat. The radio and TV play-by-play announcers might be heard to say, "He really battled up there."

These conversations with prospects who don't want to book an appointment even when you see a compelling reason to be on first base, will have the greatest long-term impact on your overall success. Why? Because these are the calls that make you resilient. The reasons why your prospect *should* book an appointment may be clear to you, but are they clear to your prospect? Does your prospect really have a problem you can solve? Would he really benefit from the same kind of solution that you have provided for others? If so, have you clearly and concisely succeeded in expressing your ideas? If not, swing again!

Here's a response you can use when a prospect declines to meet with you: "John, if you don't think it makes sense for us to meet that's fine. At the same time, I heard you say that you have some of these issues, and I'm just wondering why you wouldn't want to explore getting them resolved."

Application

The concepts and techniques offered in this chapter can be used effectively by all salespeople, whether they are selling products or services. Lets look at both types of selling, to learn more about the nuances of each.

Selling Products

For the concepts and techniques in this chapter to be applied effectively in product, technical, or complex sales, it is important that you conceptualize your product by re-imagining it as a service. You can "decommoditize" your product, and thereby differentiate yourself from your competition more effectively, if you can focus on the conceptual aspects of your solution. Here's how this works.

Let's say you sell corrugated boxes, and you have seven competitors going after the same customers. Your standard operating procedure is to quote a competitive price and hope that you win the business—at least this time. Of course, the reason you have to bid for each piece of business is that when you win the business based on price, you will lose the business the same way. It trains your customers to always look for a lower price, without regard to any of the services you offer along with the product.

What are some alternate approaches? When attempting to reach first base, here are some questions you could ask your prospect to reposition you from salesperson to solution provider:

- "Do you find it frustrating to always be switching vendors due to pricing inconsistencies?"

- "What do you sacrifice in the way of vendor creativity when you focus on price?"

- "Could a more creative vendor design a more appealing and effective package and save you money?

- Could a more creative vendor design a custom savings program with guaranteed pricing levels?"

- "How often have you been late to ship products to customers because shipments were late from one of your other corrugated vendors?"

Selling Services

Salespeople who sell services, i.e. stuff you can't see, touch, or demonstrate, sometimes suffer from the same problem: They make their solutions sound too much like products. For example, let's take a commercial-insurance salesperson, who probably tries to reach first base by asking for the expiration date of the prospect's current policy. This is the result of seeing the service offered—a solution to the client's ongoing insurance needs—as merely a product. The downside to this approach is that there will be numerous competitors vying for the same business within 30 days of the policy's expiration: not a promising situation!

What is the alternate approach? Don't wait until the prospect's policy is within 30 days of expiration: Call today! If you are an effective commercial insurance salesperson, and you have the expertise to uncover vulnerabilities, liabilities, and exposure with the current coverage, I bet the prospect would fix those problems today, rather than wait until the policy expires. Also in your favor is the likelihood that few other commercial-insurance salespeople will be competing for this business today—they're waiting for the 30-day window. With your help, the client will realize that the current vendor has shortcomings, so you won't have competition from them.

Your client, through this process, will develop tremendous respect for your expertise and understanding of his business. That's priceless.

> **TIP:** If you continue to show good judgment, expertise, and understanding, you'll do business with this client for as long as you both shall live. This is what a partnership is all about. Remember: You're not just trying to find customers. You're trying to establish long-term relationships with people who will ultimately become your partners (and your advocates).

Take a Lead

In baseball, when a runner takes a lead, he is shortening the distance between first and second base. You've gotten an appointment and you're standing on first base. Although this is an accomplishment, you still have a long way to go. In order to be properly positioned to reach second base, I suggest "taking a lead."

In sales, when we take a lead, we also shorten the distance from first to second base. Before you hang up the phone, spend two or three minutes setting up your move to second base. This will save a tremendous amount of time when you actually take off for second base. Here's how.

- Always ask for enough time. Depending upon the length of your sell cycle, the first meeting should allow enough time for you to develop a relationship and reach second base. If you have a very short sell cycle, you may be able to touch all the bases in the first meeting. Be realistic about how much time you'll need, and when scheduling the appointment, simply state, "Pick a time when you can spend 90 minutes (insert actual time needed) with me."

- Assign homework. After the appointment has been set, but before you say your good-byes, it's important to give your prospect some homework for your meeting. I suggest that you say something along the lines of, "In preparation for our meeting, it would be great if you could think about how you've been doing this up until now and, in a perfect world, how you'd like to do this in the future. That will give us a point A and a point B, and we can spend most of our time talking about what it will take to get you from point A to point B. If I can help, we can discuss what that would entail and then you can decide whether you want my help."

If you have a long sell cycle, you can modify this so the conclusion is consistent with what a first-call outcome should be. For example, if you are in technical sales you would hope, after the first meeting, to have a better understanding of the application and whether you can provide a solution. You can finish the homework request by saying, "If I can help, we can discuss what that would entail and then you can decide whether you'd like us to design a solution." "How you've been doing this" and "How you'd like to do this" are generic. You should customize those phrases so that point A represents how your prospect came to have the current problem and point B represents how things will be when the problem is solved.

For example, suppose you sell commercial photography and your prospect is an advertising agency. You would say something like, "It would be great if you could think about how you've conceptualized and arranged for your photography in the past and, in a perfect world, how that would change in order to have more creative, usable images."

Regardless of what you choose to include in this set of homework instructions, when the prospect says "OK," it assures you of a meeting during which he plans to share information with you, much like getting a batting-practice fastball to hit. A batting practice fast ball is easy to hit for a home run. If you provide effective homework instructions, the prospect will usually be ready to share the kind of problems that lead to a home run in sales.

You'll also want to take a lead from third base. For example, when you reach third base you may wish to schedule a meeting to run home. You can take a lead off third base in much the same manner as you took your lead off of first base by telling your prospect what will happen in that meeting.

Chapter Summary

Reaching first base is the first crucial accomplishment in the selling process. The more effective you become, the more opportunities you will have to score runs, build your customer base, generate referrals, introductions, and earn more money. Although prospecting is a step that most salespeople avoid and/or execute poorly, it is a simple step which, if embraced, practiced and executed will quickly and magically lift you to the top of your profession.

Where am I?

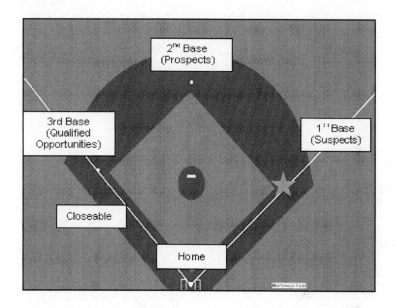

PART THREE:
GETTING TO
SECOND BASE

You know you are on second base when the prospect needs what you have, there is urgency or some other compelling reason to take action, you have developed a relationship, and he sees you differently than he sees your competitors.

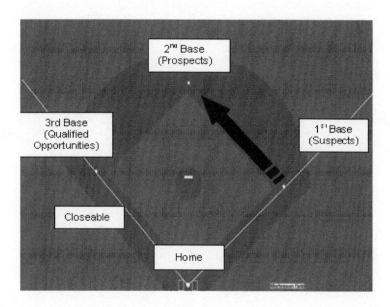

Chapter 6: On Base—The View from First

In the previous chapter, we discussed what most salespeople believe is the most difficult part of selling—getting to first base. In this chapter, we'll discuss the part of selling that requires the most skill—getting to second base. Getting to second base requires that the following three conditions be met:

#1. The prospect needs what you sell.

#2. There is urgency or some other compelling reason for the prospect to take action.

#3. You have developed a relationship with the prospect, i.e., the prospect sees you differently from the way he sees your competitors. I call this having "speed on the bases," or "the S.O.B. quality."

If your prospect needs what you sell, there is urgency, and if you have demonstrated the S.O.B. quality, you will reach second base. Let's analyze these three components in detail.

Prospect Needs What You Have

The prospect must need what you sell. Salespeople often confuse a prospect's *actual* need with a perceived need—what the salesperson *thinks* the prospect needs. Let's look at some various needs and differentiate them with some examples of what a salesperson might say to herself while trying to qualify a prospect:

- Premise: Hey, we sell those things and they buy those things!
  Conclusion: They must need them.

- Premise: Hey, we sell those things and they don't have those things.
  Conclusion: They need those things!

- Premise: Wow, they have a problem.
  Conclusion: We can help.

Only one of these examples, the third, represents a truly profitable situation for the salesperson. In fact, example three represents your best hope for higher margins, a long-term contract, and an end to bidding for every order. Why? Even though the *premises* in the first two examples may be true, the *conclusions* aren't necessarily true. In the first example, a business may be buying things they don't actually need, for a variety of reasons. For example, most of us confuse "use" with "need." I use paper clips, pens, paper, and staplers. I don't actually need them and wouldn't have a serious problem if I didn't have them. So in many cases, the act of buying does not always indicate a need. In the second example, just because a business doesn't have certain things doesn't necessarily mean it needs them. For example, a small professional services firm probably won't need a fleet management system.

If you sell a commodity, you might think that the third example doesn't apply to you. After all, you sell *things*, not solutions. But as we saw in the previous chapter, re-imagining your commodity as a solution to your prospect's problem is the key to successful selling. How do you do this?

Try asking buyers of commodities questions I call "commodity busters." Commodity-busters are designed to get your prospect to share a problem you might be able to solve. In this way, you will advance from being a supplier of commodities to a problem solver. This is a great way to start building a long-term relationship with your prospect, who will, in time, become a satisfied customer, a source of referrals, and an advocate for your business. Here are some examples of commodity-busters:

- "Why did you agree to meet with me this time given that previously you weren't interested?"

- "Has something changed since the last time we spoke?"

- "Our prices have been an obstacle for doing business together in the past, so why were you interested in speaking with me now?"

- "What happened to your relationship with XYZ Company?"

- "Working with me might require you to make some changes in your process. Will that be an obstacle?

- "We probably won't go about this the same way as XYZ Company. Are you OK with that?"

- Before we talk about ordering x446 widgets, is it OK if I evaluate whether that's even the best choice for your application??

These questions are a departure from what salespeople usually do because most salespeople are busy emphasizing the reasons a prospect should buy from them. They try to learn how low their price must be, how big the opportunity is, and various other forms of "what will it take to get the business (as presently described)?" The Commodity-buster examples I used above can totally change the nature of the opportunity. Your prospect may begin to develop an awareness that there may be some problems, not previously identified, that you are in a better position to solve than their current vendor and your competitors. When you accomplish that—and your commodity-busters will help you—having the lowest price is not usually the driving buying criteria.

I recently sat next to Mike Wagner, Business Development Manager at Rockwell Industries, on a flight to Portland Oregon. He told me that "Rockwell is never the lowest price." I attempted to clarify by saying, "You mean Rockwell is *usually* not the lowest price." He said, "No, we are *never* the lowest price.

How does a company grow to be the size of Rockwell, a $3 billion company, they never have the lowest price? If it isn't lowest price, then what is it? It is your ability to demonstrate S.O.B. Quality, a strategy I will discuss later in this chapter. Before you can use Commodity-busters to your advantage, you must believe, with all your heart that having the lowest price is *not* the key to sales success.

The Force Play

Salespeople that don't usually sell commodities have the most trouble when they encounter a prospect who wants to view their service as a commodity rather than a dynamic service. Personally, I experience this phenomenon with bankers that see training as a line item—one equally indistinguishable service that can be obtained from any vendor, without regard to content, the trainers, their expertise, their understanding of the need to create a sales culture, or their ability to create change and actually fix the problem. I have always used a technique I call The Force Play to face this challenge head on.

In baseball, when there is a runner on first base and batter hits a ground ball the infielder can throw to second base where the runner who must run to second, is "forced" out. This is called hitting into a force play.

When we use the force play in sales we describe the characteristics of undesirable prospects. This limits the prospect's ability to commoditize you. For example, in the banking sales call I would say something like, "Usually, when I talk to bankers, they have an unrealistic goal of creating more of a sales culture. They want their branch managers to make sales calls without any regard for whether the branch managers will ever leave their desks. They want tellers to cross-sell and up-sell without providing any incentive to do so and they want the trust officers to be more proactive without learning whether the people in that department have what it takes to look for and close new business. They have no structure in place to hold any of the people accountable for these initiatives and they think training will accomplish their goals."

After quickly describing my issues with this prospect I ask, "How are you different?" This forces the issue and the prospect must now explain how he is unlike those backward thinking bankers I just described. More importantly, training, at least at this bank, is no longer a line item in search of a proposal. How can you use the force play? Bookmark this example so that you can refer back to it when I discuss the S.O.B. Quality later in this chapter.

Urgency

I'm sure you've had prospects who needed what you sold and yet didn't buy from you. That's because your prospects didn't have a sense of urgency.

Let's differentiate between the various categories of urgency you might encounter while speaking with a prospect. Here are three scenarios:

- "Perfect timing—we just ran out."

- "How quickly can you get it here?"

- "This problem is costing us $1 million a day."

The third scenario is the only example of true urgency. Why? Because, in the first place, it can be quantified financially, helping to justify your price, especially when higher than the competition; and in the second place, it opens the door for you to ask "Would you like to solve the problem?" As with need, it is your problem solving expertise that will ultimately lead to a profitable relationship. The first two scenarios don't really accomplish this: They involve one-time orders instead of relationships, a quick fix that allows your prospect to go back to doing business as usual (probably with your competition). However, you can turn the first two scenarios to your advantage by uncovering the real problems, rather than the symptoms, that lie behind them. (I'll discuss this later in this chapter.)

S.O.B. Quality

You've probably had prospects with need *and* urgency who still bought from somebody else. That's because you also need the sales equivalent of what they call "speed on the bases" in baseball.

Baseball's top 10 base stealers of all time were Lou Brock, Maury Wills, Ricky Henderson, Ty Cobb, Joe Morgan, Tim Raines, Kenny Lofton, Luis Aparicio, Eddie Collins, and Jackie Robinson. These guys were not only fast and difficult to throw out, they were able to wear out pitchers who would make countless throws to first base to prevent a stolen base. At the same time, pitchers became distracted while watching these speedsters dance around first base, wondering if this was the pitch on which they would steal. The more distracted the pitchers became, the less effective they would be when they finally pitched to the batter. What did these great base stealers accomplish, besides stealing bases? They got the pitcher's undivided attention whenever they reached base.

During the 2004 American League Championship Series (ALCS), the Boston Red Sox, the first major league baseball team ever to come back from a three-games-to-zero deficit and win a seven-game series, saw their fortunes turn when speedster Dave Roberts distracted Yankee pitcher Tom Gordon, who threw a pitch right down the middle of the plate to Trot Nixon. Roberts, running on the pitch, reached third base on Nixon's single, scored on Jason Varitek's sacrifice fly, and the Red Sox' historic comeback was under way! If you have the S.O.B. Quality, you will always get your prospect's undivided attention.

If you develop a relationship with your prospect—a relationship that goes beyond seller and buyer—it is likely that he will view you differently from the way he views other salespeople. You will earn, and receive, his undivided attention, a big advantage to have over your competition.

A salesperson with the S.O.B. quality has the following attributes:

- Able to earn the prospect's respect.

- Tremendous confidence.

- Expertise.

- Asks questions that nobody else asks.

- Demonstrates excellent problem-solving ability.

- Quickly develops a relationship.

- An extremely likeable personality.

- Credibility.

- Reputation.

- Pushes back and asks challenging questions.

- Good diagnostician.

- Humility.

Notice that I did *not* say you had the best product, price, or company. If all you needed was the best product, everyone else would be out of business. If all you needed was the best price, the same companies would lose all the time. If all you needed was to represent the company with the best reputation, others would be unable to keep their doors open.

While product, price, and company can certainly be factors, they are rarely anything *more* than factors. What is essential is that your prospect chooses to spend more time with you than with your competitors—because of your interest in him, the quality of your questions, your ability to diagnose and understand his problems, your humility, your friendliness, your authenticity, reputation, expertise, and commitment to solving his problems.

Do you remember the banking example I shared when describing The Force Play? That is also an excellent example of how to establish your S.O.B. Quality.

Beating Your Competition

You may regularly compete for business among the same group of companies. In order to beat them consistently, you'll need more going for you than lower prices and your winning personality. You'll need to know as much about how they do business as possible: how they sell, what they talk about, what they think is important. You'll also need to know how your prospects perceive them.

All of this information can be very useful. Over time, you have probably learned about your competitors' weaknesses. It is your job to expose their weaknesses without badmouthing them: It is considered to be in poor

Selling Professional Services

The S.O.B. quality is a prerequisite for those who sell professional services or serve as business advisors. Bill Doerr, a sales consultant in Connecticut, says that an effective business advisor shows:

- An understanding of the client's business.

- The ability to respond to the client's needs in a professional, timely fashion.

- The ability to anticipate needs before a crisis situation develops.

- That he values his client.

- His respect for the importance and limitations on his client's time.

- His ability to protect sensitive information.

- His ability to work easily and effectively with different individuals in his client's business.

taste to say bad things about your competition, even when they are true. One way to accomplish this is with the Hidden Ball Trick.

The Hidden Ball Trick

In baseball, the Hidden Ball Trick is when an infielder pretends to give the ball back to the pitcher but keeps it hidden in his glove. The pitcher pretends to prepare for the next batter and the base runner takes his customary lead off the base. Then, without warning, the infielder tags the runner out. The play is rarely used today but often works when attempted.

In selling, the Hidden Ball Trick is an equally effective covert act of deception. Make a list of the things you say, ask, or do that you know your competitors *don't* do on their sales calls. Instead of telling a prospect that "We do such and such and they don't,"—a very distasteful way to compare companies—you can *hide* your knowledge from the prospect. Make it sound like you think your competitors actually do the same things that you do, and let your *prospects* tell you that, in fact, they don't. In the example that follows, you are discrediting your competition without ever saying a single negative thing about them. The Hidden Ball Trick can be a lot of fun!

As an example, suppose your competitors are known for making slick presentations, but not for asking questions:

You (after asking questions to demonstrate your S.O.B. Quality):
You mentioned that you were also speaking with *ABC* Distributors and *XYZ* Supply. What kind of questions did they ask you?

Prospect: They didn't ask any questions.

Result? You just enhanced your S.O.B. Quality!

Here's another example: Suppose you are in the carpet cleaning business, and before agreeing to quote a price on cleaning you always run a test to learn whether certain stains will come out. You know your competition doesn't run the test. Keep your eye on the hidden ball:

You:	I understand you are talking with Fuzzy Clean Carpet Service too. What were the results of the tests they ran on your carpets?
Prospect:	They didn't run any tests.

Gotcha! How can you apply the Hidden Ball Trick?

Challenges Getting to Second Base

As with all aspects of the sales process, you'll face challenges getting to second base. Many of them are challenges we covered in chapters 3 and 4, such as need for approval, fear of rejection, negative self-talk, overbearing ego, being an effective listener, understanding your business, and understanding why prospects buy.

What are the new challenges you must face as you attempt to reach second base?

Getting Picked Off

Perhaps you can imagine a child, after his first time reaching first base, getting picked off. It's a lot more embarrassing when it happens to a major league player, who should know better and who has a first-base coach shouting instructions. In sales, getting picked off happens when you get to first base and, even though you have as good a chance as anyone of getting the business, you don't differentiate yourself, don't ask good questions, and get eliminated.

This happens especially to salespeople who don't put forth a consistent daily effort into reaching first base and, as a result, don't reach first base very often. Most of these salespeople are convinced that although they may not be great in the prospecting department, they are superstars when it comes to closing. However, this assessment of their prowess is false. Why? In most cases, they are being unrealistic about their abilities. They think that because they close, say, 30 percent, and those who make cold calls only close around 25 percent, that they are better closers.

Well, in truth, those who close 25 percent are probably selling more than three times as much, because they're getting in front of four times as many prospects. Our 30-percent closers take shortcuts because of how good they think they are. My research indicates that this group is just as uncomfortable asking questions as they are at making cold calls. So, instead, they attempt to get to second base by making a compelling presentation. Unfortunately, that million-dollar presentation fails to get them to second base, and they get picked off first base instead. The prospects learn all they need, thank the salespeople for coming, and never take another call from them again. Eliminated!

Terry Slattery, a sales development expert in Minnesota, is a good friend and colleague, whose wonderful stories could fill a book of his own. Terry has an expression for what takes place in the scenario I just described: He calls it "premature presentation." The salesperson makes his presentation too early in the process, climaxes too soon, and everybody leaves unsatisfied. The prospect hasn't solved his problem, the salesperson doesn't have the business, and both wasted their time.

Jim Sasena, another good friend and colleague, notes that salespeople have a tendency to ask themselves "What can I do that I'm good at and comfortable with?" and not "What do I need to do to get the business." Their answer, usually, is: "I can present, I can give a demo, or I can give references." This is such a great insight, because that's exactly what happens when the degree of difficulty is compromised by the salesperson's weaknesses. If the selling situation requires the use of a challenging approach, and your weaknesses cause discomfort with the approach, there will be interference, and perhaps a collision. Rather than risk getting all banged up (psychologically, not in reality), salespeople do what's comfortable rather than what's profitable.

Lack of Patience

In sales, as in baseball, there is only one way for a runner to advance himself to second base—the tried and true method used by the greatest base stealers in the history of the game. You must be patient but quick, use the skills you were trained to use, and use them at the right time.

In baseball, a batter with patience is said to have "plate discipline"—the discipline to wait for his pitch, a pitch he can hit, rather than jumping at the first pitch that's a strike. Plate discipline, or patience, is something you must have in selling as well.

You can't close your prospects any sooner than they are prepared to be closed. While you can influence their timeline and be more efficient getting to second and third base, you still can't close them before they are ready.

The president of a large niche-manufacturer in Massachusetts told us how, as a result of his company's patience, they landed a large order 18 months after the opportunity was uncovered. This scenario is one that most companies experience, but it is a better example of persistence than it is patience.

You must be patient enough to let the process evolve, but after you've touched all the bases and closed, *not* have the patience to let your prospects put you off. It may be the single most difficult skill to balance in all of selling.

> **TIP:** Patience is not a characteristic but an art form. If you learn to master the various degrees of patience and the appropriate time for its use, your effectiveness will increase dramatically. I suggest reading George Leonard's book *Mastery* for its ability to take any discipline, in our case sales, and break it down to the basics that must be practiced repeatedly in order to achieve mastery of the concepts in this book.

Losing Touch with Reality

Salespeople who have an unhealthy need for approval are afraid to ask their prospects tough questions, so they compensate by asking insignificant ones. I equate insignificant questions to the game of 50 questions. When salespeople first learn about the importance of asking questions, they just make up a list of questions. The questions, prepared in advance, are often mechanical and irrelevant, and probably don't relate to what the prospect is saying. Since these questions cause prospects to lose patience, salespeople resort to presenting information. If the prospect doesn't react negatively to the presentation, this causes the salesperson to believe she has arrived at second base when, in fact, she still has one foot on first.

Lack of Effective Observation Skills

Your prospects will communicate to you in two ways, through their spoken words and with their body language. It's not important for you to know what any specific body language means, but it is very important for you to recognize when the prospect's body language has changed. You should specifically watch how your prospects react to what you say. For example, when a prospect who was leaning back suddenly leans forward, it is that change in body language that you must recognize. I can't tell you why it changed but we both know that something just happened. A guess could be that the prospect moved from being disinterested to interested, but it could just as easily indicate that he went from being disinterested to wanting to hurt us!

Although this ability to recognize change will be most critical when running from third base to home—while you are presenting your solution—your ability to advance from first base to second base depends on it as well. When moving toward second base, your ability to recognize these subtle changes can provide clues as to when you have identified the real problem. When your prospect moves from relaxed and conversational to more anxious and thoughtful, you are likely discovering the prospect's real problem.

Inability to Develop a Relationship

There are two components to a relationship. The first is rapport, which comes from having things in common. The second is bonding, the sense that two people have a true connection between them, a natural occurrence in families and with great friends.

Some salespeople are naturally gifted when it comes to establishing rapport, but not so gifted when it comes to bonding. So, because establishing a rapport—without bonding—comes so naturally to these salespeople, many of them are unable to quickly develop a relationship, and resort to having superficial conversations instead.

Other salespeople aren't very personable and fail to develop any rapport at all. People skills did not come naturally to me: My natural state is introverted. I am an example of someone who had to *learn* how to build rapport and develop bonding—and accomplish these early in the first meeting with my prospects. Even today, if I don't "turn on" my people skills, people might perceive me as cold, uncaring, or disinterested. But when I flip the switch and move into relationship mode, people find me likeable, sincere, trustworthy, and credible.

Bonding is much more subtle and is more of a process than an event. For someone to feel that they have a connection with you, they must be very comfortable around you, trust and respect you, like you, feel they have a common thread with you, and actually want to be with you. Notice that all of these criteria involve *feelings* rather than words—words are associated with rapport. Whereas rapport can be established in just a few minutes, it can take several meetings and many months to develop bonding. Sometimes, you don't ever bond with your prospects.

If at all possible, you should strive to develop both the bonding *and* rapport in the very first meeting with your prospects. The sooner you establish the relationship, the more likely your prospects will feel comfortable about sharing their problems.

Dale Carnegie was the first to talk about relationships and their importance in the world of sales, but he was the first to write about sales relationships in his 1936 book *How to Win Friends and Influence People.* In 1979, Richard Bandler and John Grinder, the pioneers of Neuro-Linguistic Programming™, or NLP™, published *Frogs Into Princes,* and described in great detail the skills needed to quickly and effectively develop powerful relationships with people. They were the first to talk about the powerful strategies "mirroring" and "matching".

Mirroring is the strategy of presenting yourself as the mirror image of the person you are with. Matching is the strategy of matching your voice—tonality, pitch, speed, volume and accent—to that of the other person. Both strategies, when handled subtly and effectively, cause the other person to believe that you are just like them—exactly what you want when attempting to quickly establish a relationship.

People often say that extroverts make the best salespeople and, of course, some of them are quite good. But introverts, contrary to popular thinking, make very good salespeople too. Since they don't have a goal of talking, they become very good listeners, a great attribute in sales. So, being a good talker is not necessary for establishing a good relationship.

Did you ever meet a great salesperson from the 1960s or 1970s? They had winning personalities and knew that if they could get people to like them, they could get people to buy from them. Today, relationships are as important as ever. However, a good relationship is most likely only one of several criteria a prospect might have. Price, product, value, delivery, service, expertise, appropriateness of the solution, company reputation, certifications, references, capabilities, location, facilities and plants, company size, availability, ability to customize solutions, and the willingness to place a dedicated representative inside a company are some of the additional criteria a prospect might consider today before making a decision to buy.

How I Learned to (Really) Sell

I learned to (really) sell from a career pots-and-pans salesman, Bob Jiguere, one of the top sellers at WearEver™ Aluminum from the 1940s through the 1960s. By the time he got to me in 1974, Bob was in his early sixties, and I had been with the company for just over a year, eleven months longer than most of us who began selling Cutco knives to people in their homes.

I will never forget the first call I went on with him, because it was so surprising in so many ways. First, the call was the complete opposite of the "features and benefits" selling that I had been taught to emphasize. Second…well, I should just tell you the story and you can draw your own conclusions.

We walked up to the third floor of a six-unit apartment building in Lowell, Massachusetts. We were calling on an eighteen-year-old girl who lived in the four-room apartment with her mother. Girls typically bought kitchenware for their hope chests; their mothers usually had well-established kitchen accessories. As we entered the apartment, I noticed that Bob didn't have his samples with him. But I figured he wouldn't need them, because this girl could not possibly afford a $250 (1974 prices) set of knives—never mind cookware, flatware, or china. I was sure she and her mother were destitute.

We all sat down at the table, an old gray, plastic-topped table with metal legs. Although Bob did talk with the girl, he spent most of his time talking with her mother. He asked her to make coffee and cookies and was very complimentary of her baking.

We had been in there for about 45 minutes, and if it were my sales call, I would have been finished by now. But Bob hadn't even started! He finally got around to asking the girl some questions—but why in the world was he asking these questions? "Would you like to get married?" "Would you like to have a family?" "Will you want nice things?" "Have you started putting things away?" "Do you have a hope chest?" "What's in there?" "Are you helping her, Mom?" "If you found something really special and you really wanted it, could you put aside $10 a month?" I had been taught to present and build value by asking if a prospect was impressed with what I was demonstrating. I didn't know where he was going with these questions.

Finally, he sent me to the car for the samples. He opened them but didn't demonstrate anything, didn't explain anything, didn't "build value," or tell any stories about the knives. He just opened the display and sat there looking at the knives as if they were gold bullion.

Just then there was a knock on the door. It was the girl's boyfriend, coming over to visit. I figured he was fairly possessive and jealous, because his first question was, "Who are they and what are they doing here?"

Well, the girl very nicely replied that "these boys are showing me some nice knives for when we get married."

"You don't need that shit," he said.

I knew where this call was going. We were about 10 seconds from being back in the car and going on our next call.

Bob turned to her mother and said, "These punks are all the same today. All they want to do is get in your daughter's panties."

I was going to die, right there and then. I didn't think it could get any worse, when her mother said, "You're right! I want you out of my house!"

The punk replied, "Baby, you gonna let her talk to me like that?"

The girl said, "She's right. Get out!"

Up to this point, I had been 100 percent wrong about everything that had happened. But even as I began to sense that Bob actually knew what he was doing, I couldn't have predicted what would happen next. Mom said, "I don't know how much you sell those knives for, Bob, but I'd like to get a set for my daughter—and another set for me."

Bob said, "Of course. You are one sharp cookie and a hell of a baker, too. The two sets come to just $500. Do you have that under the mattress?"

The mother said, "Oh, Bob. You know me like a book. Come on into my bedroom and I'll show you where I keep the money."

He followed; she lifted the mattress, took out a wad of cash, peeled off $500, pinched his cheek, thanked him for coming, made us finish the cookies, and wished us well.

Ninety percent bonding and rapport, a dozen or so qualifying questions, no presentation, and he sells two outrageously priced sets of knives to a mother and daughter with no creature comforts or possessions to their name. If you were on that call, would you have taken notice? I sure did. Selling would never be the same again!

Lack of Credibility

Credibility is just as important as the relationship, because prospects will not do business with salespeople who are not credible. How does one effectively establish credibility? It comes from a combination of the following factors, all of which are important:

- Believability. A prospect must find you believable. Not only is lying unacceptable, but the slightest exaggeration and over-selling of a point will likely spell the end of your chances of doing business.

- Expertise. There is more to being credible than being truthful. The prospect must believe you have expertise in your field, especially if you are conducting a technical or complex sale. The best way to establish your expertise is to ask a number of good questions that your prospects have not yet considered, causing them to answer, "I don't know."

- Authenticity. Much has been written about the importance of making a good first impression, but I believe that authenticity is equally important. While you must present yourself well, you must also look like you belong in the clothes you wear. For example, I once consulted for an investment firm that urged their clients to purchase condominiums and then rent them out for income. There wasn't much positive cash flow to these properties, and the investors' only hope to make money was an increase in value at selling time. Further complicating matters was the sales force—eight young adults, all fresh out of college, asking their prospects to invest in multiples of $125,000.

   The first thing I noticed was that they were all so uncomfortable in their off-the-rack suits. And since they were off the rack, they didn't fit perfectly. The sleeves were a bit too long or short, there was too much material under the neck, the jackets were just a bit too long or short. But they weren't uncomfortable because the suits didn't fit perfectly—they were uncomfortable because instead of wearing slacks and polo shirts they were wearing suits.

   My first order of business was to get management to allow these kids to come into the office and make their phone calls in more comfortable clothing. When they finally went on face-to-face appointments to meet with the investors, usually much older men, they were to dress nicely, even professionally, but in a way that was more appropriate for their age: dress slacks with a shirt, tie, and a v-neck sweater.

> **TIP:** Your clothes must fit you, and you must also fit your clothes. For example, when you attend a wedding, you can usually spot, within minutes, the men who pulled out their one suit jacket for the occasion. They're the same guys who don't own a pair of dress shoes and can't button the top buttons of their dress shirts. If you don't normally wear a jacket and tie, and you lack dress clothes that make you look great, you would be better off dressing in a manner that made you feel comforable.

- References. Nothing beats three great references for helping to establish your credibility, but having references can just as easily work against you. You may be too eager to share the names and might not perceive that the request for references is really a put off. The two keys are:

    #1. Never offer your references unless you are asked.
    #2. Always qualify the request for references.

Having references doesn't mean you should automatically hand them to your prospect when asked. Clever prospects will often ask for references as a stall tactic. It is much better to be certain that your prospects are sold first, and simply wish to hear somebody else tell them that they made a good decision. So how should you handle a situation when your prospect asks for references?

Why not say something like, "I'd be happy to give you all the references you need, once you've decided that you would like to do business with me. That way, we won't be unnecessarily bothering anybody and you won't be influenced by people with only great things to say about me."

Too Much Empathy

Seeing your prospects' problems from their point of view is good, but too much empathy can get in your way if it prevents you from differentiating between your prospects' symptoms, problems, and excuses. If you empathize with their symptoms, you may never get to the real problems. If you empathize with their excuses, i.e., reasons why their problems don't need to be solved, you'll never get their business. It is OK to empathize with their problems, once you've determined that they are in fact the real problems. Overcome this challenge by continuing to ask tough, timely questions. I'll discuss this further later in this chapter.

Savvy Prospects

Regardless of how long you have been selling, most of your prospects have been buying for even longer. They know how to get rid of salespeople. They have learned not to reveal their true feelings—about how interested they are, whether they are talking to your competitors, etc. Some of them have perfected the art of toying with salespeople. Most of them have a playbook, a process they have developed to prevent salespeople from getting the upper hand.

Salespeople who aren't in the top 26 percent are overmatched by these prospects. Tough prospects, if they agree to meet you, just want to know what you have, how much it will cost, and then want you to leave. If you leave, you probably won't be able to get back in to see the prospect. Dealing with tough prospects isn't as hard as it seems though. Most of them soften up a great deal once you penetrate their outer defenses. Ask the questions that you will learn later in this chapter, and you'll find that these prospects can actually be the easiest to sell. Nobody else gets to them, so you won't have any competition!

Inability to Handle Resistance

Some salespeople believe that once they reach first base, there won't be any further resistance. Others believe that the first phone call is merely a preview of coming attractions. There is no way to predict how much resistance you will encounter, but it is always prudent to prepare for *some* resistance. What are the various forms of resistance you can expect?

- They're happy:
    with their current vendor;
    with doing it themselves.

- They don't believe they have a problem:
    with the current process;
    with the current results;
    with the current product or service.

- They Don't Like Your Approach

- They Don't Like Your Company

- They Don't Like You

Of course there may also be resistance to price, delivery, quality, customer service, technical service, and engineering and design. If you are playing the game effectively though, you shouldn't encounter resistance to any of these things on your way to second base, unless you bring the issues up yourself.

Most salespeople handle resistance poorly. They start presenting facts, features, and benefits—and hope that these will turn the prospect around. If this were war, the salesperson would be seen as the enemy returning fire. You aren't perceived as a wonderful, trustworthy, expert problem solver yet. You *are* the enemy, there to take the prospect's money. When you get defensive and "return fire," it isn't good. Some prospects will think that you are arguing with them—and that is exactly what it sounds like. Others will think you started what they perceive as the hard sell because you presented information in response to resistance.

There are some prospects who will agree with your individual points but not with your final recommendation. Their disagreement often has more to do with their own resistance to change than with your solution. This scenario calls for the "Suicide Squeeze."

Suicide Squeeze

In baseball, the manager calls for the suicide squeeze in a close game, where one more run will be significant, he must have a good base runner on third base, and a batter who can handle the bat well enough to get a bunt down. It's called a suicide squeeze because the runner takes off from third base and if the batter isn't able to bunt the ball, the runner will be a dead duck at the plate.

To make this play work in selling, tell your prospect something like this: "Craig, I think you have two options. The first option is to make the decision that is most comfortable for you. The second option is to make the decision that most benefits your company (or family). Which is the better option?"

I call this the suicide squeeze because you are attempting to "squeeze" the appropriate choice from your prospect. But if he makes the wrong choice, you won't be able to score.

Most of the resistance you will face is from prospects who are happy. Let's explore this concept further. First, you must acknowledge the resistance by saying something like, "I understand you are happy with your current vendor." That shows your prospects that you are listening, and it lowers their resistance.

Prospects use the word "happy" to indicate their level of satisfaction. However, there is no universally accepted method for measuring satisfaction. In other words, we can't quantify satisfaction the way we can quantify temperature, distance, weight, height, volume, force, energy, humidity, density, size, velocity, or sound. Without a universally accepted method for quantifying satisfaction, no two people will agree on what "satisfied" means, especially not the prospect and the salesperson.

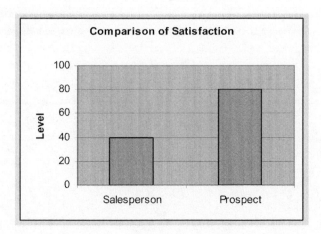

Figure 6

In figure 6, we can see a representation of this situation. A prospect, using his own scale, claims to be quite happy with his current vendor. But, if we were to use our own scale to measure his satisfaction, it would only register 40 percent compared to his 80 percent. That's quite a difference.

It's our responsibility, as professional salespeople, to help the prospect reassess his level of satisfaction, once he is introduced to our more realistic scale. Then, we will build on a powerful technique developed by Elmer Wheeler (who proffered the familiar advice "Don't Sell the Steak, Sell the Sizzle" in his 1935 book, *Tested Sentences That Sell.*) In his 1945 book, *How to Sell Yourself to Others,* Wheeler introduced a concept for handling resistant people. He called the concept "Reverse Selling," and the concept included a technique he called the "Reverse Sizzle." (Wheeler actually credited Benjamin Franklin with inventing the Reverse Sizzle; all Wheeler did was give it a name.)

Now, let's build on Elmer Wheeler's powerful Reverse Selling Technique.

The Cycle

In baseball, a perfect day for a batter would be one during which he hit for the cycle—single, double, triple, and home run. Since it is likely that our prospect believes that things are perfect, I call my powerful approach "The Cycle."

Start The Cycle by crafting five statements that clearly and concisely reflect the conditions of a customer who is perfectly happy. If he is truly happy—100 percent on our scale—what five conditions would be true? This is where your scouting report comes in handy. What are the weaknesses of the current vendor?

I'll pretend that you, the reader, are my prospect, and you are giving me—a sales development expert—resistance by telling me that sales are great and you don't need my help. That's a version of the generic "We're happy with the way we do it now."

In that case, my five "cycle statements," which would reflect 100 percent satisfaction with sales, would be:

#1. You're making more money than you ever dreamed possible.

#2. You are closing everyone.

#3. You get appointments with everyone you call.

#4. Your customers (clients) are giving you 100 percent of their business.

#5. You're working only 25 hours per week.

Review these five statements to understand how they were created. They are clear, simple, all-or-nothing, if-everything-were-truly-perfect statements.

> **TIP:** When you provide your supposedly happy prospect with five statements that would be true if everything were perfect, you can expect him to gradually realize that things are not as good as they could be.

Using the five cycle statements above as your guide, craft five cycle statements that would be true in your business if your prospects were truly experiencing perfection with your competitor or by having the service provided in-house.

Cycle Statements:

1. _____

2. _____

3. _____

4. _____

5. _____

Review your five cycle statements. They must be short. They must be powerful. They must cause your prospects to think. They must be statements that your prospect will not be able to agree with. They must not be questions. You must use the power of "always" or "never," as in "They never kept you waiting," or "They always arrive on time." You can have different statements for different competitors, products, services, and scenarios.

After you acknowledge the resistance, you can say something like: "My customers (or clients) would all say that they are quite happy too, so I assume that (insert your first cycle statement). After the prospect says, "Well, no…" you simply state, "But…" and insert your next cycle statement. If the prospect agrees with the statement say, "And…" before inserting your next cycle statement. Continue this pattern until you've offered all five statements and your prospect has not been able to agree with any, or just a few, of them.

All you have to do is become the color analyst again, summarize, and ask a question. It might sound something like this: "A little while ago you told me you were happy with your current vendor, but in the last couple of minutes I heard that results aren't what they should be. Have you lowered your expectations or have you always accepted mediocrity?"

If you have need for approval, you won't be able to ask that question. If that's the case, modify it so that you can ask something that serves the same purpose, but be a little less assertive, such as: "A little while ago you told me you were happy with your current vendor, but in the last couple of minutes I heard examples of a less-than-perfect world. Are you OK with that, or would you like things to be better?"

Joe Stolberg, founding partner in the CPA firm Stolberg & Ebbeling, and a long-time client, related this story about his use of The Cycle.

He met with two business owners who were dealing with an insurance claim. They said that unless Joe could save them a significant amount of money with the claim, it wouldn't make sense to change accounting firms.

He quickly recognized that this was a perfect scenario for The Cycle.

Joe:	It sounds like your CPA has complete control over all aspects of the claim.
Prospect:	He did not want to be involved with the property aspect of the claim.
Joe:	But I'm sure he understands that all components of the claim are interrelated.
Prospect:	It seems logical, but our CPA does not want to handle the entire insurance claim.

Joe: But I'm assuming he will represent you in the final negotiations.

Prospect: What you are saying makes a lot of sense, but we don't know the answer.

Joe said the two business owners were looking at each other as if to say, "Oh, no. How are we going to get out of this mess?"

Joe: But I'm sure your CPA maintains regular contact with you as an advisor.

Prospect: Not really.

Joe: But I'm sure you've thought about how the lack of regular advice has impacted you and your business.

Prospect: No.

Joe: Has anyone in an advisory capacity ever had a discussion on what your business and personal goals are?

Prospect: Not that we can recall.

Joe told us that the subject of saving money never came up again. Instead, the business owners focused on the value of a long-term relationship with an advisor who would be a partner rather than a service provider—someone like Joe, who would support their personal and professional goals. The two business owners became Joe's clients that afternoon.

Need to Present

If you are like most salespeople, you probably feel more comfortable presenting than asking questions. This becomes an issue when the prospect asks you to "show me what you have." If you do what they ask, it will be the baseball equivalent of running home from first base. In sales, it means you've become a facilitator—someone who just does what a prospect asks but brings no value to the table. Why do prospects ask you to present? They want to be educated and would like to compare what they've already seen to what you have. They want to get the sales call over with. They don't want to waste time with small talk. They want to get rid of you!

> **TIP:** If you do exactly as the prospect wishes, you will be in and out of that home or office as soon as you are finished presenting. Rather than facilitate, ask questions to determine what your prospect was hoping to see or hear, and then ask why that is important to him.

In the scenario with you as facilitator, you don't yet know if the prospect needs what you have, you haven't observed any urgency, and you certainly haven't given him a chance to see that S.O.B. quality in action. You haven't qualified the prospect in any way, so you can't possibly know what he can spend and what will cause him to do business with you. If we look at what you have learned about the prospect up to this point, you can't possibly present an appropriate solution—*so you must not present, period!*

If your prospect asks you to show him something, and you recognize that it's not the appropriate time to do so, what can you do instead? First, say something like: "I'd love to." That keeps your prospect comfortable enough for you to ask a question. Then you might say something like: "I'd be happy to take just a couple of minutes to tell you a little about us and the value we bring to the table, but before I show you anything, can we talk for a few minutes to see if there's anything I can even help you with?" Most prospects are agreeable to the short summary of your capabilities, and will engage in conversation to see if continuing makes sense. Once you begin that conversation, you'll be identifying their issues—and once they begin talking about their problems, they won't ask you to present again.

If your prospect rejects your offer of a short summary and conversation and repeats his request for a presentation, you will have three choices. You can present but you should ask questions as you proceed. The questions should take the form of "Does this apply here?" and "Could you tell me how?" The second option is to refuse and simply state "I'm sorry but that's not the way I work. When I present my capabilities and solutions, I want to know I'm presenting something relevant that solves a specific problem you have and that you can afford it. Otherwise I'm wasting your and my valuable time. Option three is to leave.

Prospect's Lack of Time

In the previous chapter I discussed taking a lead, and the scenario where a prospect asks you to present early in the first meeting can be avoided altogether if addressed when you take your lead. When handled effectively, taking a lead will allow your meeting to go very smoothly.

Lack of Visualization

Baseball's last triple-crown winner was Carl Yastrzemski who, in 1967, led the American League with a .326 batting average, 44 home runs and 121 RBI (Runs Batted In). He was the leader, catalyst and clutch hitter on a team that overcame 100-1 odds to win the American League pennant and advance to the World Series. In his 1990 book, *Yaz:Baseball the Wall and Me*, he wrote about his almost daily heroics during the 1967 season. A first ballot Hall of Famer, Yaz attributed his extraordinary success that summer to visualization. After each game, he would visualize every possible scenario in which he might come to the plate in tomorrow's game. He saw himself facing the pitchers that would likely appear in the game. He pictured himself hitting with men on base, with nobody out, one man out and two men out. He rehearsed every possible hitting situation, the pitches he might be thrown and he always saw himself stroking a game-winning hit or home run. He continued to visualize these scenarios through the night and into the next day until, when game time approached, he was thoroughly prepared to execute his game plan.

Most salespeople fail to visualize their calls and if they do it, they often witness a horror movie depicting their failures instead of a thriller where they play a starring role. For as long as I can remember, visualization has been a small but important part of my selling. Just prior to a first meeting, I always visualize the outcome of the selling process. Whether I expected to close a prospect on the first call or the third call, I always visualize the close; not the attempted close, the actual consummation of the sale. I always picture myself shaking hands, looking my new client in the eye and saying, "I'm really looking forward to working with you." Then I visualize how I want the meeting to begin; friendly, comfortable and easy. I imagine lots of smiles, sharing and relationship building. My calls nearly always go as planned, ending with the handshake and comment. How would you like your sales calls to play out?

Chapter Summary

In this chapter, we discussed some of the problems that prevent salespeople from reaching second base, as well as some of the things you must accomplish in order to stand firmly *on* second base. Review this chapter until you are comfortable with the material and you are able to deal with the challenges effectively.

Chapter 7: Reaching Second Base

As stated in the previous chapter, you can only reach second base if three conditions are met: The prospect needs what you sell; the prospect has urgency or a compelling reason to buy; and the prospect sees you differently from the way he sees your competitors—you have that S.O.B. quality. In this chapter, I'll show you how to determine if these conditions have been met and you'll learn powerful techniques that will enable you to pose just the right questions to your prospects. So, does the prospect need what you sell? Let's find out.

Identify Problems

In chapter 5, I asked you to identify some of the problems your prospects have had, and to identify the symptoms and reactions associated with those problems. We'll be using the results of that exercise again as we head for second base.

As you settle in for the first scheduled meeting between you and your prospect you must be prepared to learn as much as possible about him, his situation, life, and pertinent issues. A good opening line for the first meeting might be: "Did you work on my homework assignment?"

Next, you should listen for *symptoms* of the problems you solve and, as your prospect begins to share them, you should be asking questions that take you from symptoms to the real problems.

For instance, let's use sales as an example again. Suppose that the prospect expresses two issues: The first is that "sales are down," and the second is that "salespeople aren't closing".

"Sales are down" is a symptom of "people aren't closing," but the company's *real* problem is not that "sales are down." The company's real problem is that they are probably losing or about to lose money.

How can we tell? Just by asking the simple question 'why.' Frank Bettger's 1947 book, *How I Raised Myself from Failure to Success in Selling*, was among the first books to emphasize the importance of asking why. As I mentioned in chapter 4, he was also among the first to emphasize the importance of listening. Asking 'why' questions helps you to listen more effectively.

Let's try asking 'why' in the following example, to see if we can discover the company's real problem.

Prospect: Sales are down.

You: Why?

Prospect: People aren't closing.

You: Why?

Prospect: They don't seem to be any good at it.

You: Why?

Prospect: They seem to be uncomfortable.

You: Why?

Prospect: I guess they empathize too much.

You: Why?

Prospect: Their need for approval gets in the way.

We had to ask why five times to discover that the need for approval may be the problem behind sales being down.

Infield Why Rule

In baseball there is a rule called the Infield Fly Rule. This simple rule states that the batter is automatically out when he hits a pop fly to the infield with runners on base and less than two out. The simple rule becomes complex when you attempt to explain its existence. Sometimes, it's like trying to prove the existence of God. The rule is supposed to prevent a fielder from intentionally dropping the ball. Why would he do this? Well, the base runners, seeing the pop fly, retreat to the bases they were on so as not to be thrown out trying to get back to those bases. But the infielder would prefer to drop the ball—so that he can get a double or triple play by forcing the runners at the next base. So, you see it's already too complicated to explain.

I'll just go ahead and explain the Infield Why Rule, which simply states that until the prospect can no longer answer a 'why' question, we are still dealing with symptoms. It further states that you can never actually *use* the question 'why' unless it's part of a bigger question.

However, in the previous example, "why" was the only word we used in those questions, so we'll have to revise our strategy. And finally, other adverbs—such as who, what, when, where, and how—can be substituted for why. Let's try the preceding exercise again.

Prospect: Sales are down.

You: Do you have any idea why?

Prospect: People aren't closing.

You: Why do you think they're having trouble?

Prospect: They don't seem to be any good at it.

You: Why do you think they're so bad?

Prospect: They seem to be uncomfortable.

You: What do you think causes that to happen?

Prospect: I guess they empathize too much.

You: Any idea what causes that?

Prospect: They have need for approval.

There's more. Let's repeat this exercise—but this time, let's not make our prospect so smart.

Prospect: Sales are down.

You: Do you have any idea why?

Prospect: People aren't closing.

You: Why do you think they're having trouble?

Prospect: I wish I knew.

Our less-enlightened prospect can't answer all the questions, so what should we do now? The Infield Why Rule further states that when the prospect cannot answer our questions, we should ask some "Could it be?" questions to demonstrate our expertise, each followed by another "Why?" question. The dialogue would then continue like this:

You: Could it be that they just aren't very good?

Prospect: I suppose.

You: Why do you think they're so bad?

Prospect: I don't know.

You: Could it be that they get uncomfortable at closing time?

Prospect: I guess so.

You: What do you think causes that to happen?

Prospect: I don't know.

You: Could they be empathizing too much?

Prospect: It's possible.

You: Any idea what causes that?

Prospect: No.

You: They probably have need for approval.

Watch what happens as a result of the Infield Why Rule.

Prospect: That sounds awful.

You: It is.

Prospect: Can you fix a problem like that?

Increase Urgency

The second condition for advancing to second base is an urgent need or some other compelling reason for the prospect to buy what you sell. Watch how urgency is created from the continuing dialogue—as the result of asking the right questions:

You: Yes, but it takes an awful long time and not everyone is willing to change. How much time do you have to fix the problem before you run out of money?

Prospect: Only four months before we run out.

You: That's not a very long time.

Using the above dialogue, you can see how we identified both symptoms and the problem using the Infield Why Rule to create the urgency.

The Rule of Cause and Effect

The Rule of Cause and Effect states the following: "Every serious problem, if not resolved, has a serious consequence". The consequence is your key to uncovering the hidden urgency. In 1935 Elmer Wheeler wrote *Tested Sentences That Sell* and he included examples that provided a very early glimpse of this concept in action. In one example, a vacuum cleaner salesperson, after sucking up the equivalent of eight piles of dirt from a supposedly clean carpet would ask, "Where do your children play on rainy days?"

When the stunned mother answered, "Right here" the salesperson would reply, "Then this is your children's rainy day playground."

Let's build on that concept while we deal with the real problem from our dialogue—the company is losing money. How do we get to the bottom of that problem? We use the Rule of Cause and Effect. How does that work? Like this:

You:	What happens if you don't fix the problem?
Prospect:	We'll have to close.

The Hanger

In baseball, when a pitcher throws a curve ball that doesn't curve, he is said to have "hung" the pitch or left it hanging over the middle of the plate—easy to see and hit. Most good batters will jump on his mistake and hit the ball out of the park for a home run. Announcers frequently refer to this as "He threw a hanger." When a prospect shares a problem that has serious consequences—like when he says "We'll have to close"—that is the sales equivalent of a hanger. We can be confident about our ability to hit those hangers for home runs!

What is the real problem in the previous example? The company could go out of business *and* the salespeople are so bad that the company may not survive long enough to fix the problem.

> **TIP:** The key to reaching second base is not simply the use of these techniques. It is your ability to anticipate your prospect's actual problems, and to ask good, tough, timely questions that will help your prospect understand and share those problems.

Advanced Cause and Effect

The Rule of Cause and Effect states that there is a consequence to leaving serious problems unsolved, but you will want to take it one step further. It further states that "There is a monetary cost associated with every consequence". Here's how a Cause and Effect dialogue might sound:

You:	How much additional revenue will you need before you start making money again?
Prospect:	Another $3 million annually.
You:	And how long has this problem been going on?
Prospect:	Three years.
You:	So we're really talking about a $9 million problem?
Prospect:	Yes.

Nine million dollars is the quantification of the consequence. I created the Rule of Ratios to determine the ratio of the problem, in dollars, to the cost of the solution. The Rule of Ratios states that your quantification of the consequences must be at least twice the cost of your solution. For instance, the company in the example above will be able to justify a significant investment if it returns $9 million. If our solution costs $250,000 and it returns $9 million, it's a no-brainer. If, in our quantification, the problem was only a $350,000 problem, it would also be a no-brainer—they won't spend the $250,000. If we don't quantify the problem at all, it's a crapshoot. (You'll want to take note of the quantification concept, because we will use it again later in the book, when we run from second to third base.)

"Before" Pictures

Would you like an even faster and simpler method for getting to the real problem? Me too. That is why I have developed a new way to use visuals, an old tool very popular between 1950 and 1980. Originally, salespeople used visuals to tell the company story, usually at the beginning of a sales call. Today, some companies continue to tell the company story first, but they use PowerPoint® presentations instead of a prospectus. I don't encourage the use of the company story—at least not at first—unless you want to bore the "you know what" out of your prospects.

You can effectively use visuals to show images of the kinds of problems you solve. These can be photographs, graphs, charts, and other visual aids. However, make sure you only show the "before" pictures; graphs that de-

Power Point ® is a registered trademark of Microsoft Corporation.

pict *negative* financial trends; charts that show *problems*—anything you can think of that effectively *shows* a problem that you solve. The best scenario would be to have three or more visuals, and begin the sales call by asking your prospect: "Which of these images most reflects the situation at your company right now?"

You will be amazed at just how quickly you begin talking about the right issues and problems; whereas without visuals, it may have taken a tremendous amount of questioning to get to this point.

Once your prospect identifies with one of the images, you can use the techniques discussed previously in this chapter—the Infield Why Rule, the Rule of Cause and Effect, the Hidden Ball Trick and the Hanger—to create urgency and demonstrate your S.O.B. quality.

Xplane (http://xplane.com) creates powerful visual stories for large companies that have difficulty explaining complex solutions as well as large companies trying to stand out in a crowed field.

Demonstrate S.O.B. Quality

In the last chapter we spoke about having that S.O.B. quality. Among other attributes, a salesperson with the S.O.B. quality has confidence, credibility, expertise, and a likeable personality; demonstrates excellent problem-solving ability; develops a strong relationship and is able to win the prospect's respect. This gives you a big advantage over your competition.

Your ability to ask probing, insightful questions, like the ones described in the Infield Why Rule, will cause your prospect to recognize your S.O.B. quality.

Large Opportunities

Selling large opportunities is exactly the same as selling smaller opportunities, except that they produce more revenue, can be used to secure other large accounts, and are more difficult to replace if you lose them. Special challenges to closing large opportunities are the additional people who could be decision makers and the extra time required to run the bases. The single obstacle that most salespeople fail to overcome is the sense that they should treat a large opportunity differently from a smaller one.

Most salespeople become wrapped up in the *size* of the opportunity, incorrectly concluding that, because it is big, it must be a quality opportunity. As a result, they devote all of their time and energy to thinking about it. However, at the same time, they behave more passively with the prospect by failing to ask tough questions and becoming fearful of losing the opportunity. After investing months of time, and large amounts of resources and energy, they learn the business was awarded to somebody else. Worse, they don't have anything else to work on, because they stopped filling their pipeline while they worked exclusively on the large opportunity.

Treat the large opportunities exactly as you would small opportunities and continue to follow your plan.

When Things Go Wrong

Nobody is perfect. Things go wrong for everybody at some time, and you will experience this in selling too. When you recognize that things are going downhill faster than a Randy Johnson fastball, it is time to call a rain delay. In baseball, the umpires call a rain delay when the conditions are no longer suitable for continued play. On a sales call, when the conditions are no longer suitable for doing business, you can ask for what my colleague, Chris Mott, terms a rain delay. In baseball, the broadcaster and color analyst fill the time with game reviews, interviews, and chit-chat. On a sales call you can become the color analyst and provide your prospect with a little review of what just happened, where it went off course, and what it will take to get things back on track.

Chapter Summary

Let's review how to get from first to second base:

- First, the prospect must need what you have.

- Second, there must be urgency or some other compelling reason to buy.

- Third, the prospect must recognize in you that S.O.B. Quality.

- Along the way, you *must* develop a relationship.

Just follow the steps! To help you get from first to second base, you'll need:

- The Infield Why Rule

- The Rule of Cause and Effect

- The Hanger

- The Rule of Ratios

- Visuals

Where am I?

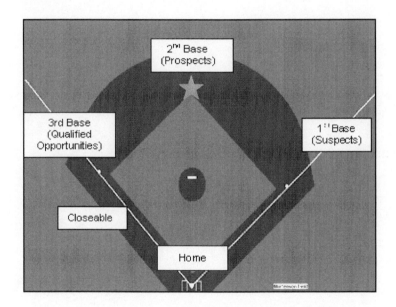

PART FOUR:
GETTING TO
THIRD BASE

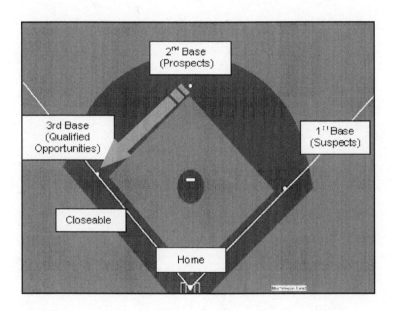

You know you have reached third base when your prospect is completely qualified to do business with you, and you are completely qualified to do business with him or her.

CHAPTER 8: REACHING THIRD BASE

In baseball, once the runner has reached second base, he is in scoring position. In other words, he can score on a base hit. When the team at bat fails to drive in the runner, this is referred to as "leaving runners in scoring position." The same two analogies can be used in sales. Some salespeople can quickly discuss all of the issues that would qualify a prospect to do business in a matter of a few minutes. Others could require several meetings with several people over a period of months to accomplish (or not accomplish) the same thing.

The point is, once you have speed on the bases and reach second base, the process of scoring from second should not be very difficult. If you thoroughly qualify your prospect, you will have fulfilled one of the two conditions for moving from second to third base, and eventually to home. If you fail to thoroughly qualify your prospect, you will be stranded on second base.

Thoroughly Qualify Your Prospect

If getting to third base means determining that the prospect is completely qualified to do business with us, there are some issues that nearly every salesperson must discuss with their prospects, and other issues that apply only to some salespeople.

My research indicates that 85 percent of all salespeople are giving inappropriately timed presentations, quotes, or proposals. This could mean they are quoting or proposing to prospects who are not prepared to make a decision at this time, don't have the money, don't plan to buy from them, or aren't ready to buy now.

Among the other areas in which prospects may not be completely qualified are as follows.

Dissatisfaction with Current Vendor

Everyone must deal with the issue of dissatisfaction with a current vendor. Your goal is either: to replace a current vendor, product, or service; or to solve a problem that no other vendor or service provider is currently addressing. In either case, dissatisfaction with a current vendor is often the buying motive. In 1965, Ralph Buzzotta, Robert Lefton, and Manuel Sherberg wrote *Effective Selling through Psychology.* In this book, the authors state that among the conditions people will experience if their problems are not solved are: pain, dissatisfaction, discomfort, tension, anxiety, worry, fear, panic, danger, loneliness, boredom, shame, resentment, frustration, entrapment, despair, futility, bitterness, and hopelessness.

Pain

Pain, one of the conditions in the previous list, was introduced as a buying motive by Elmer Wheeler in his 1946 book, *How to Sell Yourself to Others,* and is a focal point in consultative and solution selling.

Pain is often misunderstood in a sales context. Prospects don't really start out in pain, but they do have problems. When it becomes urgent for them to fix their problems, the consequences of not fixing them become painful. When your prospects are personally impacted by those consequences, then they will feel pain.

To fully understand pain in the context of selling, a salesperson must understand the difference between symptoms and the underlying problems. He next has to determine the consequences of leaving the problems unsolved. Finally, he has to quantify those consequences and get the prospect to feel pain *from the impact of the consequences.*

> **TIP:** Getting a prospect to feel pain is not required in order to have success in sales. However, if you have the ability to do it successfully, consider this a bonus that places you in the top 26 percent of all salespeople.

Willingness to Leave the Current Vendor

I've seen many examples of companies that were not happy with their current vendors but stayed with them for three reasons:

- The company's buyers liked the vendor's salespeople.

- The vendor's salespeople apologized and took responsibility for their company's shortcomings.

- The company's buyers were promised a dramatic improvement in the sales relationship with the vendor.

It is not enough merely to learn of dissatisfaction with a current vendor. You must also get a *commitment* from the prospect that he will make a change in vendors. If you can't get that commitment, there is a better than even chance that you are being used as leverage. The prospect will go back to the current vendor and say something like: "We're not happy, and *XYZ* is willing to provide better service and do it for less. See, here's their proposal." You must always avoid this scenario! How? The only way is to get a commitment that your prospect will leave the current vendor. No commitment? You're stranded on second base!

Secure a Timeline

What is the realistic timeline for getting from second base to home plate? There is mutual qualifying to be done, but that won't take very long. When does your prospect want to begin working with you? How much time do you need before you have a solution to propose and deliver? These are questions you and your prospect must ask, ponder, and resolve before you can create a realistic timeline—and from this timeline you can estimate the closing date.

Discover the Budget

Discovering the prospect's budget is a result of our effectiveness in running to second base. If we identified problems, found need, created urgency, and demonstrated S.O.B. Quality, the prospect should easily share his budget with us. If he won't, you'll never make it to third base.

Every salesperson is taught to ask for the budget, but the concept of asking for a budget is greatly misunderstood. There is much more to getting the budget than asking a question. And there is much more to establishing a selling price than receiving the budget. For instance, let's say that you have a component that will be part of a product, and you ask about the company's budget. Your prospect gives you a number, and you propose a solution based on that number. You may be surprised to learn *after* you quote or propose that the number you were given was for the entire product, not just the component in question.

There will also be occasions when there is no budget and the prospect doesn't have a clue as to what solutions like yours cost. In situations like these, you can provide your prospect with a high–low cost range by saying: "In my experience helping companies with challenges like yours, I would expect that you'll need to invest somewhere between x and y. Will you be able to do that?" If I had a preference between a prospect who had a budget that was too small or one with no budget at all, I would be more comfortable with the budget-less prospect. It's often simpler to come up with the required money when none is budgeted than it is to come up with more money when a budget has been established.

Most salespeople will need to know how much money is available to solve the problem. There are some exceptions to this, one of the most obvious being the pharmaceutical salespeople, who call doctors their decision makers but get their revenue from pharmacies.

When it comes to discovering a prospect's budget, I divide salespeople into three groups: The first group sells specific products or services; the second group sells custom solutions; and the third group sells commodities.

Salespeople who sell specific products or services usually know, by the time they reach second base, which products or services are most appropriate for their prospects, and approximately how much they will cost. These salespeople should approach discovering the budget by asking a question like: "I understand your problem and how frightening it must be to be losing $3 million a year. Are you willing to invest $85,000 to solve this problem once and for all?"

Notice that I don't recommend asking "Do you have a budget?" or "What's your budget?" These questions will often fail to work when a prospect doesn't want to share that information with you. The more direct question, asking if they are willing to invest $85,000, circumvents that problem. Also notice three more things:

- We begin the budget question by recalling the quantification of the consequences.

- We use the Rule of Ratios, i.e., the $3 million to $85,000 is significantly better than the 2:1 ratio required.

- We add the words "solve this problem once and for all." This helps your prospect associate peace of mind with the actual investment amount. I call this the Warm-Up. In baseball, the players "warm up" until they're comfortable, and we will warm up our prospect to make them comfortable about spending the money.

The second group of salespeople fits into the category of design/build selling. These are people who design, engineer, or build a custom solution for their clients. In most cases, the salesperson does not know, while standing on second base, what the final solution will be or how much it will cost. These salespeople should approach discovering the budget by asking a question like: "I understand your problem and how frightening it must be to be losing $3 million a year. What are you willing to invest to solve this problem once and for all?"

If a prospect doesn't want to share at this point, it's not a problem. Just say, "I understand, but I don't begin the proposal process without a sense of what you can afford." If a prospect doesn't know what he should budget, you can throw some round numbers out there and ask if he would be able to handle something in that range.

If you sell a commodity, you'll be asking one of my Commodity Buster questions, which might sound like this: "I understand your problem and how frightening it must be to be losing $3 million a year. Are you willing to spend a little more with me so that you won't have problems like this again?"

> TIPS:
> - Just because there isn't a budget doesn't mean there isn't any money available.
> - Just because there isn't any money doesn't mean they can't come up with the money.
> - Just because it is budgeted for next year doesn't mean they can't buy it this year.

Value Added

Today it is imperative that you add value to the sale. Value consists of two components:

#1. What you add, over and above the delivery of a product or service that provides your prospect a solution while differentiating you from your competition.

#2. That which justifies a selling price that may be higher than your competition.

Demonstrating value is accomplished through what is called the "value proposition," a formal statement that tells the world about the value you bring to the table. The value proposition is very similar to the exercises for reaching first base in chapter 5. However, there are three differences: First, you may have multiple statements for reaching base, depending on the audience, but only one value proposition; second, those statements may be more focused or targeted to a specific product or service than a value proposition; and third, your value proposition is as formalized and as public as your company's mission statement.

When you have a higher price you must be able to show one or more of the following benefits or "value added" to justify doing business with you:

- Lower total cost of ownership

- Value of your expertise

- Their relationship with you

- Additional profit they can generate

- Bragging rights

- Their customer's perceived value

- More favorable terms

- Increased sales

- Peace of mind

- Uniqueness of the solution

- Exclusivity

- Access

- Obligation

Willingness to Buy Value

If your prospect wishes to buy from the salesperson with the lowest price, and that salesperson is not you, it means you were not as effective as you needed to be on the way to second base. If you can't get your prospect to tell you under what circumstances he would pay more for the right solution to do business with you, third base will be difficult to reach. If this is the case, you must realize that you haven't truly reached second base. Why? Because you failed to find enough urgency or develop enough S.O.B. Quality to differentiate yourself. You'll have to retreat to first base and attempt to reestablish S.O.B. Quality. You can do that by summarizing your situation via one of the following statements:

- "It seems as if you don't believe I bring enough additional value to the table to justify spending a little more with me."

- "It seems as if you don't believe I understand your problem well enough to deliver an appropriate solution—even if it's a little more money."

- "It seems as if solving this problem the right way, the first time, isn't worth a little more money."

Decision-Making

You need to learn how your prospects—and any others involved in this purchase—will make their buying decisions. What are their criteria, how long will the process take, what will influence the decision makers, and how flexible will this process be?

In their 1975 book, *Using Your Brain for a Change*, psychologists Richard Bandler and John Grinder introduced the concept of Neuro-Linguistic Programming™, or NLP™. Anthony Robbins, in his 1985 book, *Unlimited Power*, simplified and popularized the concept and presented it to a much larger audience. One of the insights of NLP™ is that one can discover the internal process by which individuals make decisions—about anything—and a purchase is no exception.

In 1988, I applied NLP™ to the context of selling, as illustrated in the table below. Column one has the three NLP™ modes by which individuals communicate: visual, auditory, and kinesthetic. Column two explains how a salesperson would present to a prospect. Column three lists the ways each prospect would likely make a decision. Since most people tend to use all three modes at various times, they may not use the same mode for decision making as they would for absorbing your presentation. It is the ability to uncover the potential inconsistency between the way that a prospect absorbs information and how that same prospect makes a decision that makes understanding this particular aspect of NLP™ so powerful.

Mode	Description	How to Present	How They Decide
Visual	Emphasis on what one can see	Show them a solution using charts, pictures, graphs, slides, etc. as support.	It needs to look good.
Auditory	Emphasis on what one can hear	Tell them about the solution using written words as support.	It needs to sound good.
Kinesthetic	Emphasis on what one can feel	Make them comfortable with your solution.	It needs to feel right.

How to Present Your Solution

If you listen to the words your prospects use, you can usually identify which of the three modes your prospect prefers. Those who prefer communicating through the visual mode will often use phrases like "I see", or "I imagine", or "I can picture", or "It looks like", etc. Those who prefer communicating through the auditory mode will often use phrases like "I hear you", or "It sounds good", or "That rings a bell", or "Listen to this", etc. And those who prefer communicating through the kinesthetic mode will use phrases like "I'm comfortable with that," "Get a handle," "Massage the data," "Come to grips," "Get my hands around," etc. These phrases not only suggest which of the three modes you should use to communicate with your prospect and ask questions, but more importantly, they tell you how to present your solution.

As I said earlier, even though you identify a mode that the prospect prefers for communicating, he may not use the *same mode* for making decisions. As an example, I prefer to communicate using the visual process, and I make decisions based on how something looks. However, you may use the visual process to communicate, but make a decision based on how something *feels* to you. Thus the process a prospect uses for communicating may be different from the one she uses for decision making.

Eye movements can provide magic-like insights into a prospect's process. *Influencing with Integrity*, a book by Genie LaBorde, is a great primer on this topic.

Decision Process Rule

How then do you discover how prospects truly make their decisions? Use what I call the Decision Process Rule. This rule says that you must ask the following question on your way to third base: "The last time you did business with somebody like me, how did you know you were making the right decision?"

Your prospects' response will include a clear indication of whether their decision-making process was visual, auditory, or kinesthetic. For example, they might say "It just felt right," a definite kinesthetic response. They might say "It looked good to me," clearly a visual response. Or they might say "I liked what they had to say," which sounds very auditory.

Once you know the internal decision-making process, you know exactly what must happen in order for the prospect to buy from you. Present in the manner that is consistent with the communication mode you identified and, before you close, make sure that you meet the prospect's decision-making criteria identified in the Decision Process Rule.

Decision Maker or Makers?

Is your prospect the *only* decision maker, a *key* decision maker, or *one* of the decision makers? If your prospect is the only person who will make the decision, you can start toward third. If there are others involved in the process, you may have to meet or speak with each of them. They may not want to meet you if they don't wish to be involved in the buying process, but you must repeat the process of going from first to second base with them to learn how the issues affect each of them. When you encounter decision makers who choose not to participate in the process, simply state: "I understand the demands on their time, and I'm sure that staying out of the process has worked in the past. However, I have learned that if I get a sense of how this problem impacts everyone, I can create a more ideal solution."

A mistake that many salespeople make is believing that because they are speaking with one of the people *involved* in the decision—or worse, one of the people who will *influence* the decision—they have reached the decision maker. For instance, many salespeople whose sale involves the purchasing or procurement departments believe that the buyers make the decisions.

Although it is true that buyers have the power to say no, in most cases they merely facilitate a process that starts higher up in their organization. When you have a value proposition or a compelling reason to buy from you instead of somebody else, you have a reason to start the process with someone much higher in the organization than a buyer. Beware though—in the end, the buyer may still attempt to negotiate their best deal with you.

Ability to Make a Decision

You'll want to determine that your prospect is both the decision maker and also someone who can make a *timely decision,* i.e., to buy immediately after you present your solution. Prospects tend to make timely decisions if they don't feel the need to look at other proposals, prices, and presentations. There are two scenarios in which this can occur:

#1 Your prospect has already met with your competitors, and yours is the final presentation.

#2. Your solution is just *so* perfect that despite not seeing your competitors' offer, your prospect makes the decision to buy from you.

I wouldn't count on the second scenario happening too often, so I urge you to work on achieving the first scenario. How? In order for your prospect to make a timely decision, you will have to be the last one to meet with him. You must know that you can score on the play.

I suggest using what I call the "Rule of Lines." Have you ever been to a grocery store or a government agency when there is a long wait, and you don't want to go to the back of the line? Try asking the person at the head of the line if you can cut in front of her. (She'll tell you where to go, and it might not be just to the back of the line!)

How can you apply this concept to selling? Easy. Tell your prospect that you would really like to be the first one to present, and ask when he has scheduled your competitors. One of two things will happen. Either he will oblige—an indication that he favors you—or he'll force you to the end of the line. If he obliges, open your calendar and tell him you can't fit him in between now and the date of your competitors' appointments. Tell him you'll take a later date while acting disappointed. The Rule of Lines—it works every time!

Acceptable Solution

Salespeople sometimes propose solutions that aren't exactly what the prospect has in mind. This can be easily avoided just by asking the right questions when moving from second to third. A simple question that can help you determine whether you're on the right track might sound like: "If I were to propose a solution that included *abcdefg*, how would you react to that?" Your prospect will usually indicate whether your idea is on track or not. If they don't think it is on track, simply ask them what they would change.

Financing or Leasing Requirements

Your failure to explore financing or leasing options now guarantees a stall or a put-off at closing time. Can't you just see it? You've presented a perfect solution that didn't exceed your prospect's budget. When you attempt to close, your prospect informs you that now he'll have to figure out how he is going to pay for it, and will get back to you when he has resolved the issue.

> **TIP:** If creative funding will be an issue, it is *your* responsibility to uncover that concern before you reach third base. You must get your prospect to accept the financing, leasing, or payment terms that you can offer—or have your prospect make those arrangements now—before you attempt to score.

Commitment to Solve the Problem

In chapter 5 we talked about prospects who have a problem but decide not to do anything about it. We talked about urgency and the S.O.B. Quality as components that get a prospect to take action. But we don't want to be making guesses about whether we can score. In a close baseball game or when the team is fighting an uphill battle, a runner never attempts to advance a base unless he knows for sure he can make it safely. Likewise, we don't want to head for home unless we're sure we can score. It is important to ask your prospect, "How committed are you to solving this problem?" If they don't say something along the line of "Very committed," they aren't very committed. Go back to first base and do a better job finding the urgency using the Rule of Ratios.

Criteria to Determine a Qualified Prospect

Every company has its own policies, requirements, and qualifiers to rate prospects. Some companies, like large advertising agencies, require that prospects represent a minimum of $1 million in potential revenue. Others only sell to companies on the Fortune 100, 500, or 1000 lists. Some companies require that a prospect have a minimum number of employees. These are all size-related criteria. Does your company have any criteria of its own that would help you qualify your prospects?

Thoroughly Qualify Yourself

Getting to third base means our prospect is completely qualified to do business with us, and we are completely qualified to do business with him or her. Now that we've completely qualified our prospect, it's time to look at the second part of the requirement: Are we completely qualified to do business with our prospect?

You as Salesperson

Every salesperson must determine whether the prospect is comfortable doing business with him. Very few people buy from those they dislike, distrust, or don't respect. Fear of Rejection and Need for Approval cause most salespeople to avoid asking their prospects if they are comfortable working with them. I've heard some salespeople ask, "How did I do?" That only encourages a grade on their performance! Just ask: "Do you have any concerns with me that would prevent us from working together?"

Your Company as Solution Provider

Have you determined that the prospect is comfortable doing business with your company? Or could there be issues that would either discourage or prevent her from doing business with your company? You can incorporate this topic into the previous question. After your prospect assures you that there are no issues simply add: "And what about with my company?"

Delivery

All aspects of delivering your solution to your prospect are important. For salespeople selling commodities, this includes everything from the method you use to ship your product to whether or not you charge for shipping and handling. For service providers, this applies to the various methods of delivering your service. For instance, let's take a training company. Training companies have several ways to conduct training:

- Live in a public classroom.

- Privately in a company's classroom, hotel or conference center.

- Online via the Internet.

- Privately via consulting, teleconferencing, video cassettes, audio cassettes, CDs, interactive DVDs, or interactive Internet.

Your ability to match your delivery to your prospect's preferences will either enhance or destroy your ability to get the business.

Ability to Deliver When Needed

If you are shipping a product, the distance between your location and your prospect's location may impact the time it takes for your prospect to economically receive timely shipments. However, it can also be a factor if you need to design or manufacture a product within a certain time frame, or to deploy resources before a certain date.

I've seen it a number of times: A company asks its salespeople to "presell" its newest product. This new product gives the company a huge edge over its competitors when it has unique cutting-edge features, prospects are ripe for it, and prospects are willing to wait a little longer for delivery. The only problem with this scenario is that I've never seen a company deliver a new product when they say they will. Result? The order is cancelled, the customer is disgruntled, and the business is lost.

Ability to Provide Service

Your ability to service what you sell or, in the absence of a product, just provide service—as you promised—makes all the difference in the world. If you can do it and the prospect believes you—references are a big help in this situation—great. If you can't—and they *will* find out—it's back to second base, where you will be stranded.

Quality of Service Needed

Some customers need a level of service that goes beyond what most companies are able to provide. Whether it's the response time, the level of expertise, or the inventory of parts you have in stock, they will find out if you can't do what you promise. If, in fact, you can't deliver this elevated level of service, you will be stranded on second base.

Your Competition

Your competition's standing with your prospect is a major concern. It's one thing to know that your prospect is speaking with competitors. It's quite another to know not only where you stand, but where your competitors stand as well. Most salespeople don't ask questions that reveal the standing of their competitors. If you know who the competitors are, you can ask your prospect: "How do you feel about *XYZ?*" She may not answer, but a non-answer is also an answer. First, it tells you that she isn't comfortable sharing that kind of information with you—you are stuck on second base. Second, it indicates that you don't have "front runner status"—an important fact for you to know.

If you don't know who the competition is, now is a good time to ask. If it is not appropriate to ask directly, you can still ask something like: "If you had to choose a vendor (solution provider, firm, product, company, etc.) today, who would you go with?" If it's you, great; if not, you're back on second base, but not stranded there yet. Do you remember the Infield Why Rule? Start asking some questions.

Ability to Satisfy Prospect's Wish List

It's one thing to ask questions to identify problems you can solve. However, knowing and understanding those problems don't always provide enough information to help you create the complete and perfect solution. Most prospects have secret wish lists populated with hopes, sometimes unrealistic, that the prospect hides from the salesperson.

For example, let's say that you go to a store to select a home theater system. It would be really cool to have a ceiling mounted projector because you heard about the quality of the picture. But you also heard that projectors start at $10,000, and you only have $7,500 to spend on your entire system. It's on your wish list, but you don't want to mention it for fear of being embarrassed. Little did you know that the market just changed and one manufacturer recently introduced a quality ceiling-mounted projector for only $1750, leaving enough cash for the rest of the gear too.

Why not ask the prospect for her wish list? It's a simple question: "Do you have a wish list?" The items on the list could relate to features ("I want to be able to…"), price ("I said we have a budget of *x*, but I'd really like to solve this problem for *.75x.*"), growth ("It would be great if we could expand this thing in two years without having to start over"), control ("is there any way to lock in a price for this service, so that it doesn't go up for three years?"), or training ("I'm pretty comfortable with how these things work, but I don't want to be the one who has to show everyone else how to do it. Can you provide training?"). Wouldn't it be helpful to know the items on your prospect's wish list?

Acknowledge What You Can't Provide

How often have you been able to provide all but the smallest part of an ideal solution? For example: "We can help you deploy this in all of your offices except those in Alaska. Is that going to be a problem?" Let's learn the impact of that limitation today, before we present a solution, rather than find out later, after we've lost the business. If your prospect indicates that the shortcoming is a problem, simply ask your prospect, "How do you suggest we solve that problem?" Your prospect will usually have a better response than you, and they will usually spend money on their own solution.

Your Prospect's Criteria

Your prospect may have detailed criteria for doing business with you. We don't know what these are, and they may change from time to time, and from situation to situation. However, you must learn what these criteria are, or you may head for home plate and get thrown out! Ask the following question: "Do I have to meet any criteria that we haven't yet discussed?" You might discover a previously unmentioned criteria, such as an approved vendor list; minority or locally owned company requirements; size requirements (small business, global enterprise); offices or branches needed in specific locales, etc. As with the previous topic, if you fail to meet the criteria, simply ask the prospect how he would solve the problem.

Chapter Summary

The best part of going from second to third base is that it won't matter at all whether you are selling something technical or conceptual, if you have products or services, or if your sell cycle is long or short. The process of getting to third base should be the same for everyone! Choose the appropriate criteria and apply them consistently.

Where am I?

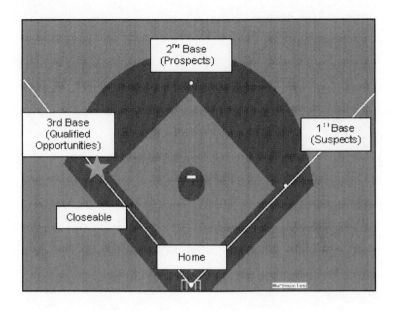

PART FIVE:
RUNNING HOME

You know it's time to run home when there is nothing left to do but present your solution. In baseball, when you are standing on third base with two outs and the batter makes contact you automatically begin running home. In sales, when you are standing on third base after completing the qualification step you are ready to run home.

CHAPTER 9: WAYS TO REACH HOME

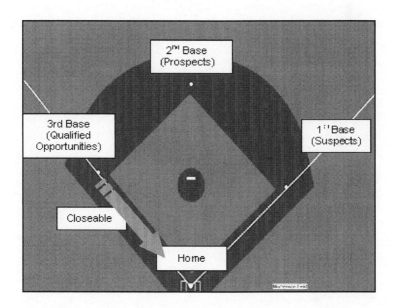

Before we make our mad dash for the plate, let's be certain that we haven't missed any of the bases. We reached first because we connected. We got to second base because the prospect needs what we have, there is urgency, and we demonstrated the S.O.B. Quality. We qualified the prospect in countless ways and are satisfied that the prospect is completely qualified to do business with us and that we are equally qualified to business with them. We must also be certain that we can effectively solve their problem, not exceed their budget, and show why they should do business with us instead of with somebody else.

The trip home can take place in a number of different ways:

- Presentation

- Proposal/Quote

- Product Demonstration

- Facility Tour

- Product Test

Most of these methods require excellent presentation skills and a tremendous ability to observe the reactions of your prospect. We'll thoroughly discuss these skills, beginning with how to present a solution.

The two biggest mistakes you can make when presenting a solution are presenting too early, as previously discussed, and failing to help your prospect understand what you are saying.

The Six Biggest Presentation Challenges

Salespeople face many challenges when it comes time to present solutions to prospects. These challenges can leave you stranded on third base, unable to score. Most have to do with communication skills—sending messages to, and receiving messages from, your prospect. I've named the six biggest presentation challenges: Ums and Ahs, Pace, Watch, Marbles, Wardrobe, and Vacuum.

Challenge #1. Ums and Ahs

No, that isn't an electrical term: You were thinking of ohms. "Ums" and "ahs" are what you say when the next thing you want to say hasn't yet reached the tip of your tongue. Can you imagine the level of frustration that baseball players would feel if after every pitch the umpire said, "Um, ah, ball three?" There is nothing wrong with silence—and when it occurs during a presentation, it may even be an asset, not a liability. Learn to eliminate your "ums" and your "ahs," and you will dramatically improve your impact.

Challenge #2. Pace

No, not the walking you do prior to being asked into the CEO's office. I am referring to the pace of your presentation. Pace refers to the way one groups his thoughts during a presentation. Here is an example. Read the following paragraph exactly as it appears:

"I'd like to start by telling you a little about our company. We've been in business since 1929 and we have a reputation for quality service and price that goes beyond what I'm telling you here because we have great people, great products, and great customers who will all tell you how wonderful we are and how well we have taken care of them over the years when it comes to solving their problems and being there when they need us and getting what they need when they need it and just being a dependable company."

That's very ugly presenting—but typical of what I've often heard. Now read the following, paying attention to the stop signs (pauses.) Notice that the basic content hasn't changed—you're still imparting the same information, but this time in a much more effective manner.

"We've been in business since 1929 (pause). We have a reputation for quality (pause) and service (pause). [Let's leave price out of this.] We have great people and great products (pause). We have great customers and you're welcome to speak with them (pause). You'll hear how well we have taken care of them (pause). Solving their problems (pause). Being there when they need us (pause). Getting what they need (pause). When they need it (pause). You'll hear how well they can depend on us."

In the second version, we have presented the information grouped by thought, so that the prospect can listen, understand, process, and remember the information. That is how you make an impression!

Challenge #3. Watch

No, not what you wear on your wrist. I mean your ability to observe how your prospect responds to your message. The prospect's eyes will convey the most telling signs. You must be able to determine whether your prospect is listening, processing information, or daydreaming. You can easily confuse processing and daydreaming, because the signs are quite similar. So follow my instructions for presenting with correct pacing, and ask as many questions as possible to prevent daydreaming. Processing—the prospect's act of taking your information and applying it to his situation—can be recognized quite easily, if you know what to look for.

Let's imagine that your prospect, a very busy CEO, is frustrated with the outdated and worn-looking furniture he has in his personal office. It reminds him of more difficult times and causes him to feel bad about himself. He occasionally recalls the time he failed to close a big sale to a prospect, the CEO of a large company. He learned that the CEO got the impression that your prospect's company was not financially capable of delivering on its promises because it appeared to lack the financial stability to appropriately furnish its offices.

So, you begin presenting your solution, and to put it into context you begin talking about how great it will make your prospect feel to sit in a chair that is appropriate for the CEO of a successful company. You go on to say that the choice of wood and finish on the desk will impress anyone who comes to visit....And it's at this moment that you notice your prospect is no longer focusing on what you are saying. He is not disinterested, but neither is he paying attention to you. He has begun processing your comments and is now imagining the scenario with the other CEO in his office—but this time it is furnished with impressive, new, stylish furniture. He begins to smile and then returns his attention to you.

There are three things that should be happening right now. First, you should have observed the information-processing taking place. Second, you should stop presenting and wait for him to finish processing. If you continue presenting, your prospect will not hear a single word that you say—he won't even realize that you are still speaking. When his focus finally returns to your presentation, you should continue or, if you want to have some fun and gain additional insight, you might ask, "What were you just thinking?"

Challenge #4. Marbles

No, not the children's game or the floor and counter top material either. I'm talking about marbles in your mouth. Record a two-minute presentation of yourself. Do you correctly pronounce words, or do you run words and syllables together, mispronounce them, and sound less intelligent than you are? If you have problems speaking clearly or pronouncing certain words, an investment in speech therapy will be very helpful.

Challenge #5. Matches

Not for lighting a fire. This time I am referring to how effectively your dress matches the dress of your audience. We previously discussed appropriate dress in the context of getting to second base (chapter 6). It is just as big of an issue when you're trying to run home. Make sure that your dress is appropriate for the presentation you will be making. If you will be visiting a manufacturing plant, dress appropriately for the plant floor. If you will be visiting a bank, pull out the dark suit and a white dress shirt and appropriate tie.

Challenge #6. Vacuum

No, not the cleaner that sucks dirt off the carpet; rather a presentation that sucks the life out of a prospect. I've seen so many salespeople go out and find problems, create urgency, and qualify their prospects—only to make an inappropriate, canned, boring presentation that is totally out of synch with the problems that were identified.

Presentation, Quote, or Proposal

Whether you make a presentation, quote, or a proposal, the components will often be quite similar. You can include any of the following 12 components if they are appropriate. (I suggest that you definitely include the first seven components for a proposal or a quote, and you may also want to consider these same seven components for a presentation.)

#1.   Cover Page. The cover page should include your company logo, your prospect's logo, and a title identifying the document as a proposal or a quote.

#2.   Cover letter. This starts "Dear Mary," and should be a friendly, enthusiastic discussion of your meetings, what you learned about her, her company and her issues, and a promise to help. Include a summary of what will follow on the subsequent pages in the form of a table of contents.

#3.   Prospect's goal. This should be your sense of what the prospect needs, why she needs it, and the questions that must be answered relative to her problems. For example: Is it realistic? Are the right people in place? Can it work? Is it the right strategy? Will people support the solution? Will the solution create any new problems?

#4.   Prospect's challenges. What challenges could hinder solving the problem? There are *always* challenges, and they should be addressed here.

#5.   Wish list. What would the prospect like to get? You don't necessarily have to deliver on her *entire* wish list, but it shows you were paying attention.

#6.   Recommendations. What exactly do you propose to do, and how will you solve her problem?

#7.   Pricing. Provide the pricing, terms, and any other appropriate information relating to price.

#8.   Justification and Return on Investment (ROI) (optional). If your prospect needs to see either of these, you should include this section here. If you need help creating an ROI strategy, ROI Calc (http://roi-calc.com) has a wonderful interactive tool that will demonstrate ROI in your business. ROI Calculator will create either a web page or an interactive PowerPoint® slide for you to demonstrate ROI to your customers and clients. You can find additional resources on calculating, building and discussing ROI at http://learnativity.com/roi-learning.html.

#9.   Company philosophy or ideology (optional). If your prospect needs to see either of these, you should include this section here.

#10.   Biographies (optional). If you are proposing a service that will be delivered by professionals, you should include their biographies here. (Please understand the difference between biographies and resumes: A biography is a record of accomplishments written in paragraph form; a resume is a compilation of work experiences.)

#11.   Samples (optional). If samples of your work are appropriate in your business, they can be included here (provide a description if they will be provided separately).

#12.   References (optional). If your prospect requested references and you qualified that request (see chapter 6), include names, phone numbers, and instructions for contacting here. You can further expedite references by registering for an account on AudioGenerator. com (http://www.audiogenerator.com) where your customers and clients can phone in their testimonials. AudioGenerator creates a simple play button that allows the testimonials to easily play on your company's web site.

TIP: One of the mistakes salespeople make with their presentations and proposals is that they suggest options, i.e., multiple solutions. Options are bad for three reasons:

#1. Options give people a reason to think things over, because they introduce confusion as to which solution is best.

#2. Options fail to differentiate you from your competition, since most other salespeople also offer options, i.e., good, better, and best.

#3. Options have the potential to destroy your credibility. If you are, in fact, an expert, asked the right questions, and learned your prospect's budget requirements, then there is only one *ideal* solution—and by showing more, you show solutions that are not the best for your prospect.

You may use a proposal to reinforce a presentation and vice versa. They are virtually interchangeable.

Request for Proposal (RFP) or Request for Quote (RFQ)

Depending on the type of business you are in, you may receive a number of requests for proposals (RFP) or requests for quotes (RFQ). A request, either for a proposal or a quote, is just like reaching first base on an error. The batter didn't succeed in getting a hit, probably didn't even hit the ball well, yet he is standing on first base via an error—a gift. The same goes for the request. You are standing on first base—not because of anything you did, but because of a gift. The problem is that most of your competitors received the same gift, and when you show up at the game, you will all look exactly the same. It is your responsibility to differentiate yourself and your company from everyone else. To do so, you can use Commodity Busters, the Infield Why Rule, and your relationship building skills.

Ultimately, your ability to differentiate yourself and your company will hinge on how well you utilize your S.O.B. Quality. Most salespeople facilitate this request by simply providing the quote or proposal and then waiting for an outcome. You establish and build your S.O.B. Quality by doing what your competition doesn't do, and what your prospect doesn't expect. You do this by using the Infield Why Rule to ask some good, tough, timely questions.

The questions should be similar to those you would ask when running to second base. The only difference here is that you are asking the questions during a time when the prospect is expecting you to be running home or submitting a proposal. Despite the existence of the RFP there is a good chance that the prospect will be unaware of the real problem behind the symptoms on which the RFP is based.

It is possible that the person you ask won't know the answers to your questions if somebody else wrote the specifications. So you'll have to learn who that was and get an introduction. Once you have the author on the phone and have identified the real problem there is one question to ask:

> "If there were a more effective way to solve that problem, and it wouldn't cost any more money, would you want to know about that?"

If you get the prospect interested in a better way, tell him you will propose this alternate solution. Two things will happen as a result:

#1. Your prospect will be anticipating your proposal because you demonstrated your S.O.B. Quality.

#2. You will be the only one bidding on the alternate solution and will likely get the business.

Cost Justification

When you sell to the government or another institution for which the buyers believe they must go with the lowest price, it often seems that your only choices are to walk away or cut your price, thereby cutting your profit. Neither is good business. The following suggestion applies if you sell solutions that don't have to be expressed in units.

One client of mine sells playground equipment to municipalities. When compared with the competition, they are always more expensive initially, but less costly in the long run because of higher quality. Unfortunately, the "less-costly-in-the-long-run" argument won't work with most government purchasing agents, because they are trained to focus on lowest cost per unit. The purchasing agents look at your price, then at the other guy's price and they conclude that the other guy can sell the same thing for less. Of course, it's not really the same thing, but the absence of criteria other than initial price allows your competition to bid a lower-quality product and often win the business as a result.

However, if you understand two things—how a purchasing agent thinks and how to perform a cost justification—you can win this business, as long as you can prove it is less costly in the long run.

Suppose you sell playground A for $55,000. Your competitor sells playground B for $35,000. The purchasing agent sees that your competitor is $20,000 less and awards him the business.

This is where the cost-justification model comes in. Your solution won't need maintenance or replacement for 20 years. The competitor's solution will have to be replaced in 10 years. While the purchasing agent doesn't care (and never will—it's not her job), she will respond to a carefully crafted cost justification. Here's how it works: You price your solution using cost per year. Done this way, your solution would cost $2,750 per year ($55,000 ÷ 20 = $2,750) and the competitive solution would cost $3,500 per year ($35,000 ÷ 10 = $3,500). In purchasing-agent lingo, you are the low bidder!

> **TIP:** If you are using the cost-justification model, you must still include a professional, third-party cost justification as an attachment to your proposal. An independent firm can create this for you after you provide them with facts and sources.

Product Demonstrations

Product demonstrations can be more challenging than many salespeople realize, because they often make many of these common mistakes:

- Failure to have all of the decision makers present.

- Failure to have a clear understanding of the desired outcome of the demonstration.

- Failure to understand the criteria for both exceeding expectations and unacceptable performance.

- Failure to have a clear understanding of the time allowed.

- Failure to understand the dynamics of the people who would likely use your product and their involvement in the demonstration.

- Failure to understand the relationship between the people who would use your product and their current vendors, i.e., the competition.

- Failure to understand the relationship between the people who would use your product and their current product.

- Failure to understand the goals of the people who would use your product.

- Failure to have a clear expectation for what will happen next.

With all that failing it's a wonder that salespeople ever get anything sold through a product demonstration. Sometimes they succeed even when unaware of the issues listed above, simply because the prospect wants and needs the product or service badly enough, the price is right, or the prospect has had a good track record with the salesperson's company. On other occasions, the salesperson knows the conditions aren't favorable, plows ahead anyway, and fails to get the business.

Following are the most important things a salesperson must do for a product demonstration to be successful.

Let the Prospect Self-Demonstrate

If you have a product that can be shown or, even better, demonstrated, *please* allow your prospect to "run it" while you provide the instructions. People become much more confident in their ability to use something new, make changes, and embrace new technology when they have had the opportunity for hands-on experience.

Demonstrate Only the Features that Solve the Prospect's Problems

If you have an exclusive feature that your competitors don't offer, you probably can't wait to demonstrate it. However new and exciting this feature may be, if it doesn't solve one of your prospect's problems, you are asking for trouble if you point it out. Why? The prospect may not want to pay for something he doesn't need, and might ask for a lower-priced model or a price reduction. He might feel that you weren't listening carefully to him. If you really want to show that exclusive feature, make sure you create the need for it by asking the correct questions when running from first to second base.

Go Slowly

A product demonstration is not a race, so if you demonstrate only those features that solve your prospect's problems, you won't need to cover as much ground and won't need as much time. Remember the importance of correctly pacing your demonstration.

Use the Prospect's Preferred Method of Communicating

Remember to present your solution using the prospect's preferred mode: visual, auditory, or kinesthetic (see chapter 6).

Use the Decision Process Rule

Use what you learned from the Decision Process Rule to achieve an end result where your prospect indicates that the solution looks good, likes what you say, or feels good about it. (See chapter 8.)

Use the Habit Quotient

People are creatures of habit, and one habit they follow consistently is that the number of times they must be asked, or closed, before they can say "Yes" is a constant. I call this the Habit Quotient. As an example, my wife Deborah has a Habit Quotient of two. In the supermarket, she'll select the second head of lettuce, the second tomato, and the second jar of mayonnaise. In the boutique, she'll choose the second sweater, the second skirt, and the second suit in her size. She never takes the first unless there *isn't* a second, and then she takes a second look. If a salesperson attempts to close her, he'll succeed on his second attempt, never on the first.

For years, sales experts have encouraged sellers to continue closing, to make that second and third effort to eventually get the business. When you apply the Habit Quotient, closing is no longer a hit or miss proposition and the attempts don't continue indefinitely. Determine your prospect's Habit Quotient by asking: "The last time you did business with someone like me, how many conversations did you have with the salesperson before you were ready to move forward?" The response becomes her Habit Quotient. Rather than equating conversations to the Habit Quotient, equate the Habit Quotient to closing attempts.

Ask Questions

Check your prospect's reactions often while presenting by asking whether something you showed or told her makes sense. Learn whether she can imagine herself using a product, whether she believes a feature solves her problem, or if she has any questions on what you covered.

Deal with Potential Objections

Most sales books have entire chapters on objections, but I haven't even mentioned them until now. That is because, if you follow the suggestions in this book, you won't get many objections, at least not until you present a solution and head toward home. What objections can you expect? Make a list of all the objections you have ever received. Then, determine which of them you might still get if you touch all the sales bases. Practice using the Infield Why Rule and the Hidden Ball Trick to deal with those objections.

> **TIP:** Norman Vincent Peale and Napoleon Hill were among the earliest to write about positive thinking and affirmations. They both wrote that what you think or say to yourself influences your actions and, ultimately, your results. A well crafted affirmation will help you turn objections into nothing more than opinions! Repeat these two affirmations: "My prospects' will have opinions about my solutions." "I effectively close prospects that have opinions about my solutions."

Move Toward an Eventual Close

The presentation of your solution is neither the goal nor the end of the selling process. It is simply a chance to show your prospect that you "get it," can solve their problem, and explain why you, more than anyone else, are the best choice.

> **TIP:** You aren't selling just a product or service: You are selling your prospect on the advantages of doing business with *you!*

Use of Audio/Visual Aids

I love PowerPoint®. The slides can really enhance a presentation, grab an audience's attention, and provide visual reference for the topic about which you are speaking. PowerPoint® slides, effectively and tastefully created, make me look bigger and better than I am.

I hate PowerPoint®. Once I've prepared the slides I have no flexibility. I can't field a question and then run with it because I don't have the appropriate slides prepared. PowerPoint® handcuffs me to my slides.

There you have both sides of the PowerPoint® argument. Most people who *hate* PowerPoint® don't know how to create slides or are limited in their ability to create visually compelling slides. Very few PowerPoint® users I've met feel the way I do about being handcuffed.

My recommendation is to use PowerPoint® when you feel it will help and to refrain from using it when you think it might inhibit your flexibility and spontaneity.

PowerPoint® Presentations

Do you use PowerPoint® to make presentations? In his book, *The Art of the Start—The Time-Tested, Battle-Hardened Guide for Anyone Starting Anything,* Guy Kawasaki says PowerPoint® presentations should follow the 10/20/30 Rule: 10 slides, 20 minutes, 30-point fonts.

Here are some more presentation tips I've come up with over the years:

- Be captivating.

- Motivate the audience to take action.

- Be clear and concise.

- Deliver the intended message.

- Ask good questions.

- Be entertaining; don't bore anyone!

- Details—not too many, not too few.

- Don't ramble.

- Don't mumble.

- Maintain a pace that your audience can keep up with.

- Connect with your audience.

- Present to the audience and not to the screen.

- Keep your audience glued to you and not to your slides.

Plant Tour

A plant tour can be a huge selling point if the activities that take place in your plant support the proposed solution. Suppose your prospect needs to purchase electronic components from an alternate vendor. Their current supplier misses deadlines, sends erroneous invoices, makes incorrect shipments, or has a chronic back-order problem. They ask for a plant tour and you can't wait to show off your new equipment. Wrong. Based on their current problem, the plant tour should emphasize organization, process, controls, systems, and the people who use them. Plant tours must be customized for the prospect in the same way as a proposal or presentation.

Product Test

The product test has many of the same criteria as the product demonstration; the most important ones relate to expectations. What constitutes a successful test? What constitutes exceeding expectations? What constitutes failure? Assuming a successful test, does that mean you get the business, and if you do, how much? If not, why not?

Chapter Summary

This chapter covered the many ways that you can run from third base to home. The common theme among these methods is your ability to agree on expectations, customize the way to communicate your solution, ask questions along the way, and understand the definition of success.

Where am I?

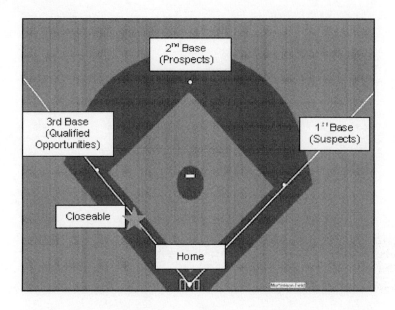

CHAPTER 10: HOW TO SCORE

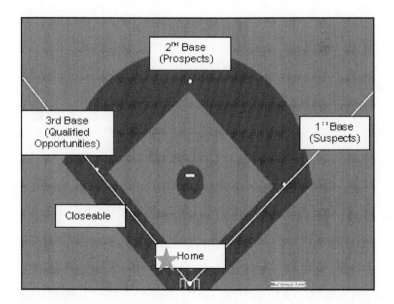

You reached first base because the prospect had a problem and wanted to fix it.

You reached second base when you developed a relationship, learned the prospect needed what you have, created some urgency, and demonstrated your S.O.B. Quality. If you did a really good job, you also quantified the consequences of the problem.

You reached third base when you completed the qualification of your prospect, covering issues like timeline, delivery, service, specs, terms, budget, current vendors, competition, your company, decision makers, decision process, ability to make a decision, whether you meet her criteria for doing business, and whether she meets any additional criteria for doing business with you.

Now you are ready to slide into home plate because your prospect reacted positively to your solution.

OK. This is the part we've been waiting for, because scoring runs is what it's all about. Winning. You have touched all the bases and now you want to cross home plate and score. Now it is time to close the deal. Here's how it works in our baseball/sales world.

Theories of Closing

There are many theories about closing, and you've probably heard most of them:

What's in a Name?

Closing has been written about so extensively that most of the closes have been given cute names, as follows: Airline Close, Alternative-Choice Close, Assumptive Close, Balance-Sheet Close, Ben Franklin Close, Call-Back Close, Concession Close, Continuous-Yes Close, Direct Close, Emotional-Appeal Close, If/Then Close, Impending-Event Close, Inducement Close, Minor-Point Close, Order-Blank Close, Physical-Action Close, Probability Close, Puppy Dog Close, Similar-Situation Close, Special-Concession Close, Summary Close, Thermometer Technique, Trial-Order Close, Verbal-Proof Close, World-Class Selling Close.

- Close early and close often.

- You are always closing.

- The close is nothing more than a culmination of a series of smaller closes.

- There is no magical event called the close.

- Always ask for the business.

- Never ask for the business.

Three Important Facts

Here are three important facts about closing which are usually not addressed:

#1. You will almost certainly succeed in closing if the following criteria are met:

A) The prospect likes you;
B) The prospect needs what you have;
C) You can solve the prospect's problem and within budget;
D) You are the only seller who meets criteria A, B and C.

#2. If you fail to meet any one of the criteria above, you may still get the business, but only after considerable negotiation, objection handling and/or tweaking of the solution or proposal.

#3. If the prospect does not like you, or you are trying to sell something the prospect doesn't need, you will not get the business.

All in the Timing

Note that nothing has been said yet about the "when" of closing. There are two equally well-established schools of thought about the timing of closing. The first school says that if you are in the act of closing, then you must get a commitment, i.e., the order or contract, now. This is especially true in the "one-call close" business like in-home sales.

The second school of thought says closing is the act of *asking* for the business. The actual commitment may not take place until after considerable objection handling, follow-up and time.

I am often asked why salespeople have so much difficulty closing. If you look at my analysis of the different selling methodologies (see Introduction), it's not very difficult to figure out. In a complex selling process, closing is defined merely as a step in a process, but not a point in time. As a result, salespeople close too early, too late, and when the timing is wrong they compensate by closing either too hard or too softly. Most often, they attempt to close before they have touched all the bases.

There is one and only one moment in time when the prospect is ready to buy. If you try to close before your prospect is ready, you'll have a battle on your hands that will negatively impact the outcome of the process. Similarly, if you arrive too late, the prospect may lose interest, patience, and/or respect for you. This could change her perception about how well you actually understood and addressed her needs.

Too many sales are lost because salespeople don't realize when the magic moment is upon them. They haven't learned when to quickly, concisely, and passionately make their final pitch and close.

Some salespeople don't close at all. They just wait for the prospect to make the first move, which, under those circumstances, is usually some form of "We'll let you know" or "We'll get back to you." Under even the most flexible of definitions, this is not closing. This is not even selling. This is presenting and passing control over to the prospect, who will gladly take it.

Consider which of the following scenarios would actually be more difficult for you to accomplish:

- Ask and answer a few more questions right now until you get the business closed;

- Go into follow-up mode, where, in a typical scenario, you'll likely have difficulty even getting the prospect back to the telephone.

Closing now is much simpler and more efficient than closing via follow-up. That can only lengthen the sell cycle, give your competition another opportunity to take the business away, and—guess what—you'll still have to ask and answer a few more questions to get the deal closed! So if you want to score, you'll have to touch all the bases and slide into home plate, regardless of whether you finish closing now, while you have the opportunity, or attempt to close later when you follow up.

Understand that most salespeople who postpone the conclusion of the close do so for three reasons:

#1. They are uncomfortable. This discomfort can be caused by letting their natural need for approval and/or fear of rejection get in the way of doing their job. The 47% of salespeople with need for approval let it interfere with closing. They become unwilling to do or say anything that might cause the prospect to dislike them, such as finish closing. The 72% of salespeople who experience difficulty recovering from rejection mistakenly take it personally, instead of understanding it for what it really is—the expression of a prospect that has not yet realized the value in the offering.

#2. 64% of all salespeople tend to think things over. If the salesperson himself needs to "think it over" when making a major purchase, chances are he will empathize with the prospect who wishes to do the same. (The "think-it-over syndrome" is the largest component of the non-supportive buy cycle, a problem when the salesperson's process for making major purchases does not support the desired outcomes of a sales call.)

#3. 55% of all salespeople haven't developed the skills to become effective closers. They just don't know what they can say that might actually work.

The Inoffensive Close

I would like to present you with what I believe is the most effective close you can use. Here's the scenario:

- We have a prospect who needs our product or service and has a compelling reason to do business.

- The prospect is perfectly qualified to do business with us and we are equally qualified to do business with the prospect.

- We have the perfect solution, based on the prospect's budget and time frame.

In other words, you've touched all the bases, rounded third base, and are on the way home to score. Assuming that your solution solves a business or a personal problem, the only thing you have to ask is some version of "Would you like my help?"

You can customize that question so that it is more specific to her problem and your solution, but here are the important things to remember about the question:

- It is totally inoffensive.

- It does not sound like a closing question.

- There are only three possible answers: "Yes," "No," and some form of "I'm not sure."

What must happen for that question to work? You have to touch all the bases. The question won't work if you haven't, and that's what's so great about it. The process of touching all the bases supports the question; and in turn, the question, which won't work if you don't touch all of the bases, thereby supports the process.

So let's put the question in perspective. Most of this book, almost every single word, has been written to help get you into scoring position, just so that you can ask, "Do you want my help?"

Here's how the Inoffensive Close works. If the prospect agrees to do business, you cross home plate without a throw being made and you win! If they don't agree and either say "No"—which is very unlikely at this point—or give you some version of "I'll think it over," a throw has been made and, in *very* slow motion, the play will develop and you will learn whether or not you will score.

This closing situation has all the suspense of a tie game, bottom of the ninth inning, the base runner sliding into the plate, the throw coming in from left field and the play too close to call. "Here comes the runner, here comes the throw and he's...."

Now here's the slow motion part. Since getting the prospect closed could conceivably take quite some time, we may be sliding into home for 20 minutes or more. We will use the Inoffensive Close, only this time I will share the complete process with you.

Potential Problems

If you have followed the process and touched all the bases, you will not have to deal with any of the following problems. They include, but aren't limited to:

- Don't need it

- Can't afford it

- Staying with their current vendor

- Issues with your company

- Unacceptable terms

- Not impressed with your solution

- Not ready

- Need to test it

- Relationship with current salesperson

- Can do it themselves

- Unwilling to change

- Not important

- Can't get approval from decision maker(s)

- Delivery isn't fast enough

- Price is too high

- Comparing proposals

- Waiting for another price

The discipline of touching all the bases eliminates most of the usual issues that arise at closing time, but there are still some we haven't eliminated. Which issues remain possible? Only these:

- Need to discuss with the other decision makers.

- Any form of "I'll think it over."

Now that we are in context and you understand how unlikely it is that you will hear any objections at closing, let's unwrap the entire Inoffensive Close and watch what happens.

Three Questions

There are a total of three questions that make up the Inoffensive Close. They must be asked verbatim and in this exact sequence:

#1. "Do you believe I understand your issues, your problems, and your concerns?"

#2. "Do you believe I/we have the expertise to solve your problem effectively?"

#3. "Would you like my help?"

You ask the first question and the prospect answers "Yes." You ask your second question and the prospect answers "Yes." You ask your third question and your prospect says "Yes." Game over. You win!

But what happens if your prospect answers "No" to your first question? You are in a jam. The entire outcome hinges on these three questions and your ability to get your prospect to answer "Yes." And remember, if you truly touched all the bases, how could your prospect possibly answer "No" to question #1? But let's assume for a moment that she does. She is telling you that she doesn't think you understand her issues, her problems, and her concerns. Can you recover from that?

Sure. Use the Infield Why Rule and the Hidden Ball Trick and begin asking some "Why do you feel that way" questions. It could simply be a misunderstanding. If that's the case, apologize, review the issues as you understand them, and then restate your first question. On the other hand, maybe you did fail to understand her issues, problems, and concerns, in which case you have most likely lost the game.

Handle a "No" response to your second question in exactly the same manner as above. Assuming that your prospect answered "Yes" to your first and second questions—she believes you understand her issues, problems, and concerns, *and* have the expertise to solve her problem—what are the chances that she'll say "No" to your third question? Almost none.

Realistically, we are dealing with the likelihood of either a "Yes" or an "I'll think it over." You already know what to do with a "Yes," so I'll discuss the "I'll think it over" with you.

> **Warning**: When your prospect wants to think things over, the only one really thinking it over will be you.

Window of Opportunity

In most cases, you will have a very small window of opportunity to close the business. Issues tend to capture your prospect's attention for a very short period of time. Once you have presented, attempted to close, and failed, the prospect is likely to be on to the next important thing in his life or business.

> **TIP:** Your ability to influence your prospect diminishes in direct proportion to the time that has passed since your attempted close.

If you weren't able to persuade him to do business with you when you were in front of him—with solutions on the table, problems still unresolved and competitors unable to contact him—what are the chances you can successfully persuade him to do business with you at a later date, without all of those advantages?

It becomes extremely important for you to recognize that you get only a single optimum closing opportunity—and this is it, right now! If you don't get it closed now, you will have very little chance of getting it closed later. You must use all of your strengths, skills, desire, commitment, total determination, and focus to close this deal while you have the chance. It is your responsibility as a professional salesperson. That is the only outcome for which you are compensated. You aren't paid for visits, relationships, presentations, or attempted closes—just signed contracts!

You might be wondering when I will stop lecturing and finally give you some techniques for overcoming "I'll think it over." The reality is that the techniques won't work until you are convinced that you must get your prospect closed at this point in the process. Without total conviction on your part, there is no chance that any technique will accomplish that outcome for you.

Are you ready?

Rule of Triple Elimination

When a prospect says she wishes to think it over, use my Rule of Triple Elimination and make the following three assumptions:

Prospect: I'll need to think about this.

You: Obviously, I failed to convince you that this was the best solution for your problem.

Prospect: No, quite the contrary. I think this is a very appropriate solution.

You: Then I must have misunderstood your budget.

Prospect: No, this was well within our budget.

You: Well, if it's an appropriate solution and it doesn't stretch your budget, the only thing left is me. You must not be comfortable with me.

Prospect: Actually, I like you a lot.

You: Well I don't get it. If you like me, like the solution and it didn't stretch your budget, why aren't you letting me help you?

The Rule of Triple Elimination gives you three opportunities to eliminate the indecision. It also prompts your prospect to say aloud that she likes the solution, price, and you. Hopefully, that's all she'll need to do in order to realize that there isn't anything left to think about. Do you remember the Habit Quotient from chapter 9? If your prospect has a Habit Quotient of two, the second attempt should be enough to get her closed. But what if your prospect's Habit Quotient is three? We continue.

You:	It sounds like there isn't anything we can do to get this wrapped up today.
Prospect:	That's right. I always need to think about it.
You:	I understand. It's a habit.
Prospect:	That's right.
You:	Can you explain what you do when you think it over?
Prospect:	I'll review your proposal and make a decision.
You:	Can we compromise?
Prospect:	Perhaps.
You:	What if I go outside while you think it over and you can call me back in when you're ready?

Those of you with need for approval are already getting uncomfortable, because you are scared that your prospect will become upset with you. I explained in chapter 3 how to overcome that, and you can't let it get in the way now.

Those of you with a tendency to think things over will also feel uncomfortable. You will empathize with the prospect and fail to understand how thinking it over will be a problem for you.

What happens if the third attempt fails to get your prospect closed? What if her Habit Quotient is four? Ask your prospect the following: "I have a question. We both know that you need my help. Let's just pretend for a minute that you had actually said yes to me today. What is it about saying yes that would have scared you?"

> **TIP:** As long as the prospect is still answering your questions, you are still selling and getting that much closer to closing the business.

If you are like most salespeople, you probably give up long before your prospects do. My research shows that 74 percent of salespeople give up too soon. However, you don't have to remain in the bottom 74 percent. You can choose to become one of the top 26 percent or, even better, one of the elite 6 percent today. The biggest difference between the strong and weak salespeople is their ability to close a deal when the prospect isn't quite there yet. Remember what I told you in chapter 5 about the fine art of patience. This is when you must be patient enough to allow your prospect to arrive at the same place as you, but not so patient that you will accept "I'll think it over."

Prospect: You know what? You're right. Let's get this done!

Price Objections

My clients have so few price objections that this section was an afterthought! And while you won't have many of them either, I figured it is better to be safe than sorry.

When a prospect states a price objection—for instance, "It's too much" or "It's too high"—there is no way for you to know, without asking a question, what she really means. Your first challenge is to determine which of the possibilities listed below is the one to which your prospect is referring. Use the Infield Why Rule and ask a question like, "What exactly do you mean?" to find the real issue.

- It's more than they thought it would be. This is not necessarily a bad thing. As a matter of fact, you can actually ask your prospect, "Is that good or bad?"

- It's more than they can afford. This is a problem. However, if you touched all the bases as we discussed, you should have learned what they could afford on your way to third base. If you exceeded the budget they gave you, shame on you. If you are within their stated budget and now they can't afford it, that's a different story. State, "I must have gotten my wires crossed somewhere along the line. When we spoke two weeks ago, I thought you told me that your budget was bigger than this."

- It's more than they *want* to spend, even though they can afford it. In this case, the money is there but they don't want to part with it. Use the Hidden Ball Trick and simply state, "You must have found a comparable resource, expert, and solution for less." If you were effective running to second base, this won't be true.

- It's more than they think the solution is worth. This is a little more difficult to deal with. As an example, let's say I wished to obtain a baseball autographed by Pedro Martinez. I would have four methods of obtaining a ball like that:

  1. I could wait with an unsigned ball outside a team parking lot and hope that he signs it for me—for free.
  2. I could go to a memorabilia shop or website and pay the fair market value, which, in January 2005, was $400.
  3. I could attend a local charity auction and bid on the ball at a silent auction and get it for $500 to $600, while helping a local organization.
  4. I could attend a big, black-tie dinner gala to benefit a big-name charity, bid on the ball at a live auction and get it for $1,000 to $2,000, while helping an even bigger organization.

     The point is that worth, or value, is so subjective. You must use the Rule of Ratios and review the numbers with your prospect. It would sound something like, "Perhaps you could help me to better understand the problem. When we spoke a number of weeks ago, I was under the impression that this problem has cost you around $9 million over the last three years. And now, I think you're telling me that the $9 million return is not worth the $85,000 solution. Can you explain how you came to that conclusion?"

- It's more than somebody else's price. This is actually the simplest to handle of all the price objections. First, you'll have to learn who had the better price. Then, we can use a technique I call Leveling the Playing Field. You would state, "Let's level the playing field for a minute and assume that everybody you are speaking with has the exact same solution and the exact same price. Who would you go with?" This temporarily takes the emphasis off of price and places it on the salespeople and their companies. If you were effective running to second base, the answer should be you. If it isn't, you will have a very difficult time overcoming a price objection. It's one thing to spend more money to do business with the vendor of choice. It's quite another to spend more money to do business with the vendor of little desire. If the prospect does choose you, then we can use the Infield Why Rule to learn her reasons for preferring you. From among those reasons, you should be able to identify one or more that is not true of the vendor with the lowest price. Use the Infield Why Rule and ask, "Are you willing to sacrifice that for a lower price?"

- It's more than you told them it would be. There goes the credibility, trust, respect, integrity, and honesty you were supposed to build on your way to second base. The time you spent inquiring about your prospect's budget on your way to third base was wasted as well. If you actually let this happen, you don't deserve the business.

- It's more than the last time they bought it. These things happen, and that should have been covered by the time you reached third base. In this case, apologize for not letting them know earlier and ask if it will be a problem.

- It's what they always say when they hear *any* price the first time. They are bluffing. The question then becomes, is this a prospect that needs to win, or is she just testing to determine if there is a better price? In baseball, a runner will draw a throw from the pitcher to check out his pick-off move. We can use the same technique, Drawing a Throw, to find out what the likely scenario is here. Simply state something like, "I'm sorry. I should have told you earlier that we don't apply discounts. Is that going to be a problem?" The prospect that is just checking to see if you can do better will let you know it's not a problem. The prospect that needs to win will let you know it *is* a problem. Ask what would make her happy, and then, find out what will happen if you can get that discount approved.

Other Decision Makers

This obstacle should have been dealt with on your way to third base, where qualifying your prospect included learning who the decision makers are and how the decision-making process works. Don't make this mistake twice. Since you won't get this business right now, there are three steps to follow if you want to close it sooner rather than later:

#1. Acknowledge the situation. Tell your prospect that you totally understand and respect his need to speak with the other decision makers.

#2. Treat the decision makers individually. Tell your prospect that you "understand that he can't speak for the others, but if there weren't others in the decision-making process what would have happened?" The prospect in front of you right now must be totally sold and committed to you and your solution if he is to convince the others to buy from you. If he is not completely sold, you'll have to use the Rule of Triple Elimination until he is either sold or you determine that he can't be sold.

#3. Get a concrete date and time for follow-up. Once you are convinced of his commitment to you and your solution, you'll need to find out what he plans to tell the others. Make sure he is strong enough to persuade the others! Ask him what he thinks will happen. Then, learn when the conversation and decision will take place and plan a specific day and time to follow up for a decision.

Crossing the Plate!

The final score, from Corporate Headquarters Field, Salespeople win a close one by the final score of 1-0.

Getting All of the Business

If getting the order is akin to hitting a home run, then getting all of the business is like slugging a grand slam. The process presented in this book makes it very easy to hit a grand slam. If the prospect has a problem you can solve, then the problem is likely a chronic one. Giving you a single order probably won't solve the customer's problem, at least not the way it would if he gave all of his business to you. It's your responsibility to understand this dynamic and talk about the big picture—not just the single piece of business that is on the table.

Most salespeople attempt to win future business by senselessly repeating an abbreviated version of their selling process over and over again as new opportunities arise. This may lead to the development of a good relationship with the customer or client. However, the constant quoting and proposing reinforces the buyer-seller relationship, and the salesperson never rises to the level we attempt to create in this book—becoming a partner or trusted advisor in your field of expertise.

How does one get all of the business? An effective approach is to use a technique I call the Table Setter.

The Table Setter

Let's build on another idea from Frank Bettger's 1947 book, *How I Raised Myself from Failure to Success in Selling.* Bettger introduced the idea of "the sale *before* the sale," and he called it the Monkey's Fist, based on the nautical term for a weight secured to a line and thrown from a docking ship to the pier. I've adapted and improved the concept and renamed it the Table Setter. In baseball, the batters at the top of the batting order are called table setters. It's their job to get a rally started by reaching base. The Table Setter is a very appropriate term for referring to the sale that will help you get the rest of the business. To understand my Table Setter technique you must conceptualize it as the sale *after* the sale.

Setting the table is all about setting expectations. It is what most salespeople would like to accomplish but they don't know how to communicate the concept to their customers so that it achieves the desired result.

Here is what you should say *after* the first sale has been completed: "I believe it would be mutually beneficial for us to help you with all of your business, and there may be some very compelling advantages for you. Perhaps this first piece of business will provide you with a good sense of what we are all about, give you an opportunity to learn about our customer service, attention to detail, great inside people, technical expertise, and problem-solving ability. After you've had a chance to gain some experience with us, can we discuss what it will take to help you with all of your business?"

Chapter Summary

Closing is all in the timing—there's a brief window of opportunity—and it occurs after you have touched all the bases. Once the magical moment is upon you, the simplest means of closing is the Inoffensive Close. If you've touched all the bases using the techniques described in this book, you've placed your prospect in a position where the simple question "Would you like my help?" will be answered with a resounding "Yes!"

Any remaining obstacles—the need to discuss the purchase with other decision makers or some form of "I'll think it over"—are rare at this point but can be handled by the Infield Why Rule, the Habit Quotient, and the Rule of Triple Elimination. Each of these techniques will help you take advantage of the optimum time to close: right now!

Where am I?

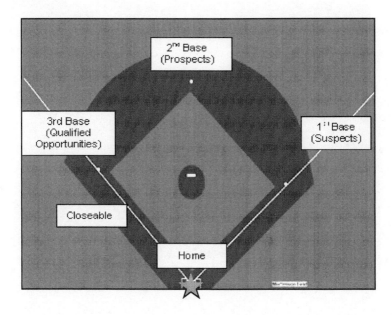

Chapter 11: Account Management

The subject of account management could be another book in itself—and probably will be! I would like to discuss four facets of account management that relate to sales.

The first facet deals with selling throughout the organization. When managing large accounts it is important for you to think both horizontally and vertically. In other words, you need to think about selling at all levels of the organization, as well as to other departments, divisions, districts, regions, subsidiaries, facilities, branches, plants, and offices.

There are two requirements to effectively sell into the rest of the account: introductions and shortcuts.

The introduction is your shortcut to other opportunities. It is equivalent to a walk—a free pass to first base! It is not enough to ask for names. Your customer must make the introduction for you—a phone call or a personal introduction. In the introduction, she must explain her business relationship with you, the problems you have solved, the value you bring to the company, and perhaps a reason why this peer should meet with you. Just make sure you call within 24 hours of the introduction, so that you will not have any difficulty getting through or reaching first base.

Here's a mistake that many salespeople make. They get the free pass to first base, but then they fail to touch the rest of the bases. They become over-confident and believe they don't have to work as hard to get this business, because of the power of the introduction. Nothing can be further from the truth. The introduction gets you to first base and nothing more. You must do the work from there and use this process just as you did to get the previous orders from this account. No additional shortcuts allowed.

The second facet of account management concerns follow-up visits and how you should handle future opportunities.

If you have achieved the status of partner or trusted advisor, you can work with your customer to handle each piece of business as it comes along, providing prices as requested. If you have not achieved partner status, then you must never simply quote a price. That's being lazy and ineffective, and it will cause you to lose your advantage. Sure, this is a current customer, but you are always starting from first base. Why? Each opportunity is different, and you must repeat the process of getting from first to second base. The run from second base to third base need not be as thorough as the first time, but you'll still need to cover some of the issues again, especially those related to budget. Finally, you will have to run from third to home as you did the first time. Failing to pay attention to the details while running down the third-base line could result in your being thrown out at home.

The third facet of account management concerns account maintenance. In today's highly competitive environment it is more important than ever to protect the business you already have by preventing your competitors from taking it away from you. Whether you choose to take your clients out for breakfast, lunch or dinner, have a simple meeting at their office, or invite them to a more prestigious event, you must meet with your customers on a regular basis. Use these meetings as an opportunity to show your appreciation for their business, ask if everything is going as expected, learn of any problems and, when they exist, fix them immediately. Everyone makes mistakes. You will be judged by how you respond to your customers and solve their problems. This is also a good time to learn what you could be doing better, learn of new sales opportunities within this account and get introductions to opportunities in other accounts. Finally, it's always a good idea to prepare your prospect for what your competitors will be doing to take this business away from you. Here's an example of some dialogue that always seems to work:

You: You know Bob, there are a lot of companies in my
            industry that aren't doing as well as we are. From what
            I hear, some of them are getting desperate. Can I ask
            you a question?

Customer: Sure.

You: What will happen if one of their salespeople stops by and says that they can do what we are doing—but for a lot less?

At this point you've prepared them for what will likely happen at some point in the future, but framed it in such a way that they associate a low-ball offer with desperation. Most customers will tell you that there is no way they would look at an offer like that; but some, clearly the minority, will tell you they would have to "seriously entertain the opportunity." When this happens you can use the following dialogue:

You: I thought you were happy.

Customer: We are.

You: In all the years I've been helping people like you, the only time a customer ever thought about doing business with somebody else was when there was something I wasn't doing for them. What am I missing?

By now, you'll discover if there is something missing from your deliverable, or whether your customer is truly happy.

> **TIP**: It is much easier to solve a customer defection problem *before* the situation presents itself than after.

The fourth aspect of account management concerns getting referrals and introductions to potential opportunities from outside an organization. There are seven steps required before you have earned the right to ask for a referral.

The first step is to create a four-column table, listing your customers or clients in the first column. Label the second column "relationship", the third column "expertise", and the fourth column "influence."

The second step is to examine your personal relationship with each and every customer. If you have a strong personal relationship, enter an "A" in the second column. If your relationship is good but not great, enter a

"B" and if your relationship is fair at best, enter a "C". It is important to be objective when conducting this exercise.

Step three requires that you honestly assess the degree to which they value your expertise. If they believe that you walk on water, enter an "A" in column three. If they believe you have helped them a lot, enter a "B" and if they believe you've helped them a little or some, enter a "C".

In step four, highlight the customers that you were able to grade either "A" or "B" for both relationship and expertise. These are the customers from whom you have earned the right to ask for referrals. Identify the customers where your grade for relationship is a "C" and set out to improve those relationships prior to asking them for referrals. Similarly, attempt to add more value to the relationship by offering quality advice to the customers where your grade for expertise is a "C".

Step 5 requires you to identify customers that you would guess are centers of influence. Use "A" if you are sure they are, "C" if you are sure they are not, and "B" if you don't know.

The fifth step is to ask for referrals from the appropriate customers. Here is some dialogue that always seems to work.

You: Have I met or exceeded your expectations?

Customer: Yes.

You: I was hoping you would say that yet I'm a bit con-
            fused. Since you haven't referred me to any friends
            or colleagues it has caused me to question whether or
            not you were truly happy.

Customer: We're very happy but you never asked for a referral.

You: Then it's my own fault. I'm sorry. Can I ask now?

Customer: Sure.

You: Who could I help the way I have helped you?

Your customer may be able to provide you with a name right now or might have to get back to you. The seventh and last step is very important. When your customer says that you should speak with Mary Smith, ask your customer if she can phone Mary for you, tell Mary about how you've helped, and ask Mary if she'd like to speak with you. Your referral has become an introduction.

TIP: Until you have received an introduction, all other leads and referrals are simply cold calls where you know a little about the prospect.

Chapter Summary

Account Management is not difficult, but surprisingly, the majority of salespeople do not practice it consistently or effectively. You must plan for it by anticipating the problems, opportunities, and challenges you will encounter, and proactively use the appropriate strategies. The recurring business from established accounts can provide a firm foundation from which to expand your business. Make sure that you don't become complacent or distracted when you should be hustling down the first-base line.

APPENDICES

Appendix A: Percentage of Salespeople Who Have the Issues We Identify

Issue	%	Description
Makes excuses	60	Whether the salesperson takes responsibility for results.
Need for approval	47	Whether the salesperson seeks the approval of prospects and customers.
Non-supportive buy cycle	64	Whether the salesperson's process for making a major purchase supports the selling process.
Self-limiting record collection	84	The collection of beliefs or records that either support or sabotage the selling efforts.
Discomfort talking about money	53	Ability to have an in-depth financial conversation with a prospect.
Tendency to become emotionally involved	52	Whether the salesperson can stay in the moment or starts talking to himself during the call.
Difficulty recovering from rejection	72	How long it takes to recover from an incident where the individual is rejected.
Lack of goals, plan, or tracking	83	Whether the salesperson has written goals, a written sales plan to reach those goals, and a tracking system to be assured of success.
Too trusting of what prospects say	86	Salesperson accepts everything the prospect says at face value.
Lack of self-esteem	40	How the salesperson feels about himself.
Poor time management	45	How effectively the salesperson manages his time, territory, and appointment schedule.
Won't prospect	50	Whether the salesperson will voluntarily prospect for new business.

Not money motivated	56	Whether the salesperson has the incentive to earn more money than he is making at present.
Lack of killer instinct	55	Whether the salesperson has that instinctive ability to know when to close and close effectively.
Low money tolerance	33	Whether the amount of money the salesperson considers to be "a lot" is in fact a lot.
Vulnerable to Prospects who wish to think it over	64	If a salesperson thinks things over before making a purchase.
Vulnerable to prospects who wish to comparison shop	93	If a salesperson is a comparison shopper.
Inappropriate quotes or proposals	85	If a salesperson places more value on the quote or proposal than whether the prospect is ready to do business.
Calling on a buyer too early in the process	53	When the salesperson doesn't begin the process with the decision maker.
Not uncovering the real budget	40	When the salesperson uncovers the budget, but it turns out not to be the real budget.
Wasting time due to ineffective use of or no actual selling system	97	If the salesperson is wasting time with people who will not do business with him.
Unable to get past secretaries or gatekeepers	50	Whether the salesperson can get the decision maker to the phone on a cold call.
Not prospecting consistently	60	Whether the salesperson is prospecting on a daily basis.

Taking put-offs	93	Whether the salesperson is taking the stalls and put-offs the prospect gives him.
Too much talking	58	When the salesperson is talking more than listening.
Ineffective use of questions	36	When the questions being asked do not serve the purpose of further uncovering the issues and qualifying the prospect's ability to do business.
Not asking enough questions	58	When the frequency of questions is too low.
Inappropriate follow-up	92	When the salesperson allows himself to be put into follow-up mode because of a failure to close at the appropriate time.
Inappropriate presentations	84	Whether the salesperson is making presentations prior to the point where he has a qualified prospect who is ready to make a decision.
Ineffective handling of people	57	When the salesperson is not able to deal with multiple persons and loses control of the call.
Not getting appointments	33	Whether the salesperson has success booking appointments when prospecting.
Not getting commitments	40	Whether the salesperson is getting appropriate commitments from the prospect before proceeding.
Not developing bonding or rapport early enough in the process	74	Whether the salesperson can quickly develop a relationship with the prospect early in the first meeting.
Not reaching actual decision maker	68	Whether the salesperson is getting in front of the final decision maker, the one who makes, rather than contributes to, the decision.

Appendix B: The Six Sales Methodologies Versus Baseline Selling

The following table provides a snapshot of the six sales methodologies and their inherent strengths and weaknesses, compared to the Baseline Selling.

Approach	Concept	Pros	Cons
Feature/ Benefit	Product centered	Requires only product knowledge and presentation skills.	You had better be good at handling objections.
Consultative	Needs centered	Used effectively, creates tremendous urgency and positions seller as an expert.	Difficult to learn and execute;. learning to create pain is a pain.
Relationship	Relationship centered	Make lots of friends, and people buy from their friends.	Lengthens the selling process.
Strategic	Politics centered	When you know what you should say and to whom, you have a strategic advantage.	But how do you get them to buy from you?
Solution	Solution centered	Causes seller to be viewed as a solution provider rather than a vendor.	Difficult to learn and execute; not enough emphasis on closing.
Customer	Customer centered	Causes prospect to feel he/she is in control and not being manipulated.	Salesperson as merely a facilitator.
Baseline Selling	Solution centered	Easy to learn and implement.	None.

Appendix C: Definition of Baseball Terms as Sales Metaphors

Term	Baseball Meaning	Sales Meaning
Home Run	A hit ball that leaves the playing field in fair territory. The batter can touch all the bases and score a run.	You got a big piece of business.
Grand Slam	A home run hit with the bases loaded, i.e., runners on first, second, and third base.	You got all of their business.
Single	A hit ball that is not caught in the air and not misplayed, allowing the batter to reach first base.	You got to first base because you made "contact."
Pitcher	The player who throws the ball to the batter.	Your presentation consists of a series of "pitches."
Closer	The pitcher who enters late in the game to preserve the win.	You take on the closer role to close the business.
Walk	The pitcher throws four pitches that are not strikes, and the batter is awarded first base.	You got to first base via an introduction or a referral.
Hit by Pitch	The pitcher hits the batter with the pitched ball, and the batter is awarded first base.	You got to first base because the prospect targeted you, rather than visa versa.
In the Field	The team playing defense.	Going on sales calls.
Sacrifice Fly	A fly ball, usually to an outfielder who catches the ball; the runner on third base beats the throw home and scores a run.	You "connected" really well, but the prospect used you to keep a competitor honest.

Term	Baseball Meaning	Sales Meaning
Sacrifice Bunt	The batter gives himself up by bunting, or pushing the bat toward the pitched ball, getting thrown out at first base while the other runner or runners move up a base.	You offered something for free as a means to getting on first base, and this back-fired.
Pick-Off Attempt	An attempt by the pitcher to catch a base runner off the base by throwing to the fielder, who attempts to tag the runner out.	The competition took a shot at you and failed.
Picked Off	When the runner is tagged out during a pick-off attempt.	The competition got you "thrown out."
Caught Stealing	The runner attempts to steal the next base, usually second base, but is thrown out by the catcher.	You got on base but at-tempted to move the process along too quickly and got "thrown out."
Foul Ball	A batted ball that is outside one of the two foul lines.	You "connected" but didn't get to first base.
Strike Out	The pitcher throws three strikes to the batter, who fails to put the ball in play.	You failed to reach first base.
Reached on an Error	A batted ball is misplayed, allowing the batter to reach base.	Everyone is safe—every-one received an RFP or an RFQ.
Made the Cut	A player, attempting to make the team in spring training, is not released or sent to the minor leagues, thereby making the team.	Prospect narrowed the field and you're still in the run-ning.
Score	A base runner scores a run.	You got the business.

Term	Baseball Meaning	Sales Meaning
Intentional Walk	The pitcher intentionally throws four balls, putting the batter on first base, thus preventing the batter from potentially causing more trouble by stroking a big hit.	Prospect has a major problem, invites you in, and tells you about the jam they're in.
Blown Save	The closer fails to preserve the win.	You blew the close; you lose the business.
Bullpen	The area where the relief pitchers watch the game and warm up.	Room where salespeople make calls to prospects.
Heavy Hitter	A hitter who hits for power—often hitting home runs.	Top salesperson.
Scoring Position	A base runner is on second or third base.	A position from which you can win the business.
Rain Delay	When play is halted because of rain.	You call "time out" because the conditions are no longer acceptable to continue selling.
Getting Booed	Fans boo a player for poor performance, or simply because he is on the visiting team.	Your prospect doesn't like you.
Color Analyst	The broadcaster who analyzes the plays.	When you provide a real-time analysis for your prospect on what's happening in the call as you see it.
Touch Base	The expression used to describe the action of a base runner as he crosses a base.	An appropriate time to follow up.

Term	Baseball Meaning	Sales Meaning
In a Pickle	When the base runner is caught between bases, and the fielders are throwing the ball back and forth in an attempt to tag the runner out.	When the salesperson gets into a jam and needs to get some coaching.
Third-Base Coach	The coach who often gives signals to the batter, telling the batter whether to swing, bunt, or just take a pitch. The third-base coach also signals the base runners heading to third base and home, advising them as to whether they should keep running or stop, slide or stand.	The person who can give you coaching with regard to the prospect you are calling on and how to more effectively get the business.
Taking a Lead	The base runner takes a few steps off first base to shorten the distance between first and second base.	The salesperson shortens the distance between first and second base by giving the prospect some homework.
Batting Order	The order in which nine players will come to the plate to bat during the game.	The order in which salespeople get to meet with the prospect to make their presentations.
Table Setter	One of the batters at the top of the order, who must get on base in order to get a rally started.	The first piece of business the salesperson does with a customer that leads to further business.

Term	Baseball Meaning	Sales Meaning
The Hidden Ball Trick	Fielder pretends to return the ball to the pitcher but keeps it and hides it in his glove. When the runner takes a lead, the fielder tags him out.	The salesperson asks the prospect questions about the competition that he already knows the answer to, in order to get the prospect to discredit the competition for him.
The Force Play	Base runner is forced out at the next base by the infielder who fielded a ground ball.	Prospect is forced out of his routine by the salesperson who describes a typical undesirable prospect and asks this prospect how he is different.

Appendix D: The Four Bases of Selling—Techniques for Running the Bases

Technique	Base Path	Description
The Inoffensive Close	Home	The simple three-question close.
Taking a Lead	Getting to First	Setting up the first appointment so that you are closer to second base at your first meeting.
The S.O.B. Quality	Getting to Second	That special quality of yours—expertise, questions, presence, trustworthiness, etc.—that causes your prospect to pay more attention to you than to your competition.
The Infield Why Rule	Getting to Second Scoring	You must keep asking "Why" questions until you can no longer ask a "Why" question. You can't merely ask "Why?" but you must ask questions that serve the same purpose as asking why, how, what, when, or where.
The Rule of Cause and Effect	Getting to Second	There is always a reason for your prospect's symptoms, and this rule says you must find it out.
The Rule of Ratios	Getting to Second	The cost of the prospect's problem must be at least twice the cost of the solution.
The Cycle	Getting to First Getting to Second	When your prospect is "happy," this is a five-statement routine to help him recognize that he may not be as happy as he think.
The Hanger	Getting to Second	When your prospect describes a problem that allows you an easy swing at the consequences.
The Visual	Getting to Second	Graphs, slides, charts, or pictures of your prospect's likely problems.

Technique	Base Path	Description
Commodity Busters	Getting to Second Getting to Third	Questions that differentiate you from your competition when you are selling products that your prospect views as commodities.
The Warm-Up	Getting to Third	Use the Rule of Ratios to warm your prospect to the idea of spending a lot of money.
The Rule of Habits	Coming Home	Every prospect will say "No" a certain number of times before he can say "Yes."
The Rule of Triple Elimination	Scoring	The three statements you would make to a prospect who needs to "think it over."
The Table Setter	Scoring	The first piece of business you do with a company that will lead to getting all of a company's business—a grand slam.
Decision Process Rule	Getting to Third	Ask the following: "The last time you did business with somebody like me, how did you know you were making the right decision?"
Rule of Lines	Getting to Third	Technique for arranging to be last in the line of salespeople presenting solutions.
Hidden Ball Trick	On Base	Technique for getting the prospect to tell you about the weaknesses of your competition.
Suicide Squeeze	Getting to Second Running Home	Technique for getting prospect over their resistance to change.

Technique	Base Path	Description
The Rule of Contracts	Running Home	When bidding, use cost per year (based on a cost justification), instead of cost per unit, to get the attention of purchasing. Done this way, the high-priced solution can be the low-cost bid winner.
Leveling the Playing Field	On Base	When in a competitive pricing situation, you can level the playing field by asking who the prospect would do business with if everyone had the same price.

Appendix E: Salesmind

Most salespeople need help overcoming the head and stomach problems that skills training won't solve. Many sales trainers ignore this part of development because they don't know how to help people overcome these weaknesses. Those in the know wish they could bottle and ship the solutions, because they are so time consuming. In the spirit of "if we could only bottle and ship it," *Salesmind* helps salespeople overcome the following obstacles:

- Need for Approval

- Fear of Rejection

- Call Anxiety

- Low Money Tolerance

- Getting Emotionally Involved

- Discomfort Talking About Money

- Not Being Goal Orientated

- Low Self-Esteem

- Lack of Killer Instinct

- Excuse Making

Salesmind is available for both the computer (self-hypnosis) as well as Audio CD (affirmations).

You can order *Salesmind* at: http://www.objectivemanagement.com/salesmindinfo.htm

Mindless Selling

My first book, *Mindless Selling*, starts with the assumption that you don't lack the know-how, and explains why salespeople often can't put what they know into practice. Through stories and case histories, you'll learn what differentiates a sales superstar from a sales dud. And you'll learn—with specific instructions, exercises, and additional reading material—how to overcome hidden weaknesses once and for all.

You can order *Mindless Selling* at:
http://www.objectivemanagement.com/mindlessselling.htm

Appendix F: The Baseball Diamond—The Four Bases for Success

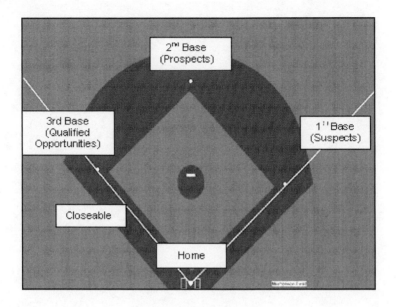

Reaching First Base
Got an appointment

Second Base
Need what you have
Urgency
Relationship
S.O.B. quality

Third Base
Prospect is qualified in every way
You are qualified in every way

Running Home
Presented a solution that is both budget- and needs-appropriate

Appendix G: The Baseball Diamond as Timeline

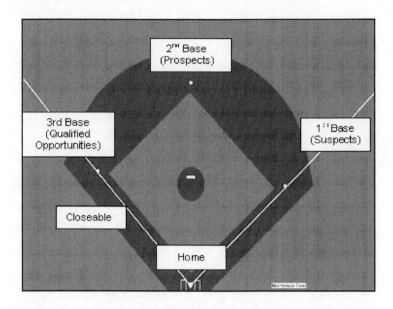

First-Base Line—Suspects
Got an appointment

Second-Base Line—Prospects
They need what you have
Urgency
Relationship
S.O.B. quality

Second to Third Base—Qualified Oppportunities
Prospect is qualified in every way
You are qualified in every way

Third-Base Line—Closeable
Presented a solution that is both budget and needs appropriate

Appendix H: The Baseball Diamond—Visual Pipeline

For an updateable electronic version of the visual pipeline, visit:
http://www.baselineselling.com

BIBLIOGRAPHY

Bach, Richard	Jonathon Livingston Seagull	Avon	1976	
Bandler, Richard and Grinder, John	Frogs Into Princes	Real People Press	1979	
Bandler, Richard and Grinder, John	Using Your Brain for a Change	Real People Press	1985	
Bettger, Frank	How I Raised Myself from Failure to Success in Selling	Simon & Schuster	1947	
Bosworth, Michael	Solution Selling	McGraw-Hill	1994	
Buzotta, Lefton, Sherberg	Effective Selling Through Psychology	Ballinger	1965	
Carnegie, Dale	How to Win Friends and Influence People	Pocket Books	1936	
Dyer, Dr. Wayne	Your Erroneous Zones	Avon Books	1977	
Farber, Steve	Radical Leap	Dearborn Trade	2004	
Hill, Napoleon	Think and Grow Rich	Combined Registry Co.	1937	
Jolles, Rob	Customer Centered Selling	Free Press	2000	
Kanter, Rosabeth Moss	Confidence: How Winning Streaks and Losing Streaks Begin and End	Crown Business	2004	
Kawasaki, Guy	The Art of the Start: The Time Tested, Battle Hardened Guide for Anyone Starting Anything	Portfolio	2004	
Kurlan, Dave	Mindless Selling	AuthorHouse	2001	
Kurlan, Dave	Salesmind	Subconcious Training Corp.	2001	Audio
Laborde, Genie	Influencing with Integrity	Sytony	1983	
Leaman, Dr. Kevin	Growing Up First Born	Dell	1989	
Lee, Bill	The Wrong Stuff	Penguin	1985	
Lee, Bill	The Little Red (Sox) Book: A Revisionist History of the Boston Red Sox	Triumph	2003	

Lee, Bill	Have Glove Still Traveling: Stories of a Baseball Vagabond	Crown	2005	
Leonard, George	Mastery	Plume	1992	
Mandino, Og	The Greatest Miracle in the World	Frederick Fell	1977	
Meyer, Paul	The Power of Goal Setting	Success Motivational Inst.	1960	Audio
Millman, Dan	No Ordinary Moments: A Peaceful Warrior's Guide to Daily Life	H.J. Kramer	1992	
Millman, Dan	Body, Mind Mastery: Creating Success in Sports and Life	New World Library	1990	
Millman, Dan	The Way of the Peaceful Warrior	H.J. Kramer	1980	
Morgan, Sharon Drew	Selling with Integrity	Berkley Press	1999	
Nightingale, Earl	The Strangest Secret	Keys Company, Inc.	1956	Audio
Peale, Dr. Norman Vincent	The Power of Positive Thinking	Prentice Hall	1952	
Rackham, Neal	SPIN Selling	McGraw-Hill	1988	
Robbins, Anthony	Unlimited Power	Free Press	1985	
Stone, W. Clement	The Success System That Never Fails	Prentice Hall	1962	
Wheeler, Elmer	How to Sell Yourself to Others	Dell	1947	
Wheeler, Elmer	Tested Sentences That Sell	Prentice Hall	1935	
White, Wendall	The Psychology of Dealing with People	The MacMillan Company	1936	
Williams, Al	All You Can Do Is All You Can Do and All You Can Do Is Enough	Ivy Books	1989	
Yastrzemski, Carl	Yaz: Baseball the Wall and Me	Doubleday	1989	
Ziglar, Zig	Goals - How to Set Them, How to Reach Them	Nightingale Conant Corp	1989	Audio

About the Author

Dave Kurlan is the Vice President of Objective Management Group, Inc., the industry leader in sales assessments, and the CEO of David Kurlan & Associates, Inc., a consulting firm specializing in sales force development. He possesses 30 plus years of experience in all facets of sales training, sales management and consulting.

A regularly featured Conference attraction, Dave has been a top rated speaker at Inc. Magazine's Conference on Growing the Company, the Sales & Marketing Management Conference and DCI's Sales Management Conferences.

Internationally known for his ground breaking work in evaluating sales people, he is the developer of The Dave Kurlan Sales Force Profile, a tool for evaluating sales forces, co-developer of Salesmind, software that helps salespeople overcome their weaknesses, and co-developer of SalesTrack, a web application that helps sales managers coach and hold their salespeople accountable.

He has been featured on radio, television and in print, including features in Inc. Magazine, Selling Power, Sales & Marketing Management Magazine and Incentive Magazine. He is the author of Mindless Selling and STAR, a proprietary recruiting process for hiring great salespeople. He is featured on Inc. Magazine's video How to Increase Sales and Profits by 1000% and was a contributor to Dan Seidman's book, The Death of 20th Century Selling.